THE
2025
EVOLUTION GUIDE

THIS GUIDE BELONGS TO:

_____

EMAIL:
_____

PHONE:
_____

IF LOST, PLEASE RETURN.

THE
2025
EVOLUTION GUIDE

CRAFT YOUR PATH: A YEARLY GUIDE TO SOLAR TRANSITS IN HUMAN DESIGN

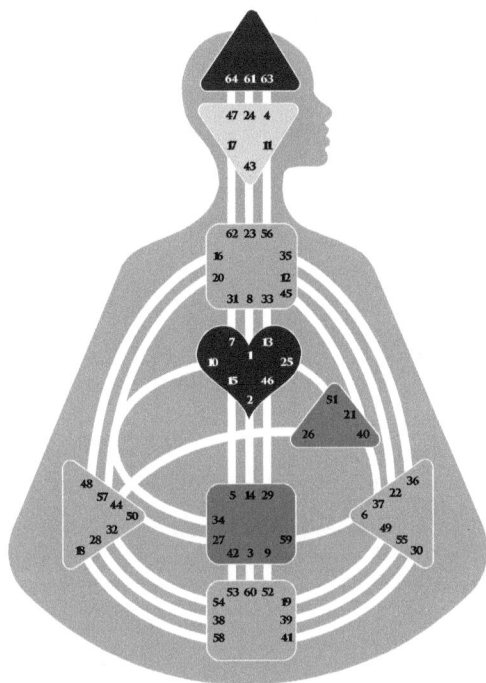

DR. KAREN CURRY PARKER

2025 Quantum Human Design Evolution Guide:
Using Solar Transits to Design Your Year

Quantum Living Press

Quantum Alignment System, LLC

2112 Broadway St NE Ste. 225, #305, Minneapolis, MN 55413

www.quantumhumandesign.com

www.freehumandesignchart.com

Email: support@quantumhumandesign.com

A Library of Congress Control Number has been requested and is pending.

ISBN (Paperback): 979-8-9910244-2-6

Books may be purchased for educational, business, or sales promotional use.

For bulk order requests and price schedule contact:

support@quantumhumandesign.com

First Edition 2024

QUANTUM LIVING
PRESS

DEDICATION

To all my students, Quantum Human Design Specialists, and Quantum Alignment System™ Practitioners: Thank you for trusting me to be your teacher. Thank you for sharing the gift of Who You Truly Are with the world. I am because you are. I love you!

HOW TO USE THIS BOOK

The 2025 Quantum Human Design Evolution Guide is a workbook with a weekly writing assignment, affirmations, and Emotional Freedom Techniques (EFT) setup phrases. If you are not a fan of journaling, feel free to contemplate the prompts in whatever way works for you. You may walk with them, meditate on them, or even discuss them with your friends.

I am excited to share with you the updated Quantum Human Design language. Over the years it has become obvious to me that the vocabulary in Human Design is in need of an upgrade in response to evolutionary shifts and with respect to new research that shows how the language we use is so powerful, it can even change your DNA. I hope you enjoy the new language!

The Quantum Human Design Gates and planets have a "challenge" associated with them. This is what you must master to get the most out of the movement of the Sun, which occurs approximately every six days. Before you complete the writing assignment, read the "challenge" for each Gate and contemplate what you need to do to get the most out of each of the weekly archetypes.

This year, we've included the earth transits to help you explore how you need to nurture and ground yourself each week. The energy of the Earth helps you stay aligned and supported so that you can better accomplish the themes highlighted by the Sun. In addition to the solar contemplations, you'll find a short contemplation or exercise to help you stay grounded and nurtured during the week, based on the theme highlighted by the Earth.

This year, we've also added Mercury Retrograde cycles. You'll learn about these key cosmic "pauses" that invite us to go inward and realign with our Voice, our message, and our relationships.

The Emotional Freedom Technique is a powerful energy psychology tool that has been scientifically proven to change your emotional, mental, and genetic programming to help you express your highest potential. Each week, you may work with a specific EFT setup phrase to help you clear any old energies related to the archetype of the week. (Learn more about how to use EFT here: https://quantumhumandesign.com/intro-to-eft)

You will also find exercises for each new moon, full moon, solar eclipse, and lunar eclipse, which are complete with a writing/contemplation assignment and affirmation. You'll be guided in working with the theme of the lunar cycles and eclipses so that you can make the most of these powerful energy cycles.

Every Human Design year gives us a 365-day creative cycle that supports us in releasing what no longer serves us, allows us to consciously increase our creative energy, grow, and evolve with the support of the stars.

May you have a prosperous and joyful 2025!

OTHER BOOKS AND RESOURCES
BY DR. KAREN CURRY PARKER:

Understanding Human Design

Human Design Workbook

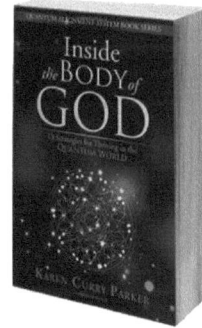

Inside the Body of God

Introduction to Quantum Human Design 3rd Edition

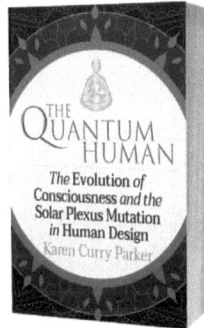

The Quantum Human: The Evolution of Consciousness and the Solar Plexus Mutation in Human Design

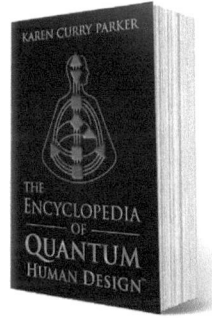

The Encyclopedia of Quantum Human Design

https://quantumhumandesign.com/karen-curry-parker-books

CONTENTS

INTRODUCTION

INTRODUCTION

This book is a weekly guide designed to give you a deliberate way to harness the energy of the Sun and the Moon to support you in creating what you want in your life.

Quantum Human Design is a collection of cross-cultural, ancient, and modern archetypes. An archetype is a pattern of thought or symbolic image that is derived from the past collective experience of humanity.

We experience all of the archetypes in the Human Design charts, either from our own unique charts, our relationships, or through planetary transits. In other words, we all have all of the chart. We just experience the archetypes of the chart differently depending on the unique configuration of our individual charts.

The colored-in or "defined" elements in your Human Design chart tell you which archetypes you carry in your own chart. The "defined" elements in your chart are part of what you must conquer to bring your gifts into the world. These energies represent your soul curriculum, what you're here to learn over the course of your life.

The white or "undefined" elements in your Human Design chart tell you a lot about what you are here to learn from others and from the world. You will experience these archetypes in a variety of different ways depending on who you are with and what energies are transiting in the celestial weather. The undefined elements of your chart represent the themes you are designed to explore through your relationships with others and your interactions with the world.

Over the course of a calendar year, the Sun moves through all 64 of the Human Design Gates. The Human Design Gates contain the energy code for 64 core human archetypes. As the Sun moves through an archetype, it "lights up" that theme for everyone on the planet, creating a theme for the week.

We all deal with the weekly themes. Even if the theme doesn't impact your chart deeply, it will impact the charts of the people around you. The gift of solar transits is that they give you an opportunity to work deliberately with all 64 of these core human archetypes and consciously focus on living the highest expression of these energies in your daily life. The solar transits also bring you creative energies that help you meet the goals you set for yourself each year.

The moon in Human Design, represents the energy of what drives us. In traditional astrology, the new moon phase and the full moon phase represent bookend energies that mark the beginning and the end of a monthly creative cycle.

The new moon helps us set the intention for our goals for the month. The full moon supports us in releasing any energies, beliefs, or blocks that are hindering the completion of our goals.

Lunar and solar eclipses are bookends that mark beginnings and endings. The work we do in between can be powerful both internally and externally. Eclipse energy represents cycles that support you in aligning more deeply with your bigger goals in life and breaking free from habits and patterns that keep you from growing and expanding.

To learn more about the transits and how they affect your personal Human Design chart and your energy, visit:

https://quantumhumandesign.com/understanding-solar-transits

2025 THEME

KEEP ADJUSTING YOUR ATTITUDE
AND FLY TOWARDS THE HORIZON.

Welcome to 2025!

The nature of the Universe is to evolve. Change, growth, and evolution are constants in the human story.

This creates somewhat of a conundrum for most of us as we are deeply conditioned to be certain. We want to be right. We want rewards and recognition for having the answers. We long for predictability and, to a certain degree, the ease that certainty brings. If you know what is certain, then you can plan accordingly.

Uncertainty is destabilizing. It makes it hard for us to prepare for what's next. It makes us worry that we'll fail or that we won't be able to do what we want - or need - to do.

But, uncertainty is an essential part of the growth process. We stagnate if everything stays the same. Without cycles of disruption or upheaval, we run the risk of never evolving. Even nature requires disruption to stay fertile. Pine forests require fire to open pine cones so seeds can be spread. Volcanoes and floods eventually create fertile soil.

The key to surviving uncertainty is knowing how to artfully navigate through change. While the outer world is in flux and shifting, we must know how to stabilize our attitude. To do this, we must be clear on who we are and what we value. Without these two factors, it can be difficult to know our position in relation to the horizon, and we run the risk of falling out of the sky and losing momentum.

The age of materialism is over. We are at the dawning of the quantum era, a creative revolution of such importance that it will rival the scientific revolution in its historical impact and importance.

We are at the downturn of a systems growth cycle and at the beginning of a new growth curve. We've outgrown systems that no longer serve us while simultaneously growing into new ways of creating the world. We've been at this crossroads for about a hundred years, but we've reached the hardest part of this evolutionary process.

Think of it like this: Systems have growth curves. When we come to the end of a growth cycle, we trend down on the curve. Things fall apart and what used to work doesn't yield results anymore. This part of the growth curve is chaotic and disruptive, but is essential to creating fertile ground for new growth.

At the same time, evolutionary systems are emerging and starting a new growth curve. There is much innovation and momentum in this new cycle. But, like all new cycles, there is learning, exploration, and, often, failure as part of the new growth. New patterns are emerging but haven't been proven to be effective and established enough - yet - to trust and build on them.

These two cycles overlap each other, creating a crossroads in time. The old systems are dying, and the new systems are emerging. The planets show us that this crossroads is at its peak between 2024 and 2027. During this time, there is collective and often personal conflict. Some of us want to go back to how things "used to be." Some of us want to move forward into the new.

The dilemma is that we can't go back and are not quite ready yet to move forward. I like to call this liminal part of the growth cycle "The Void." It's easy to lose our way forward when we're in the Void. We can get lost in the chaos and the grief of leaving the past behind while we struggle to define where we're headed and what path to take forward. It's easy to feel lost and confused during this natural part of the growth process.

Knowing how to navigate the Void is essential to the growth process. Those of us who understand this crucial part of transformation know that we have the capacity to influence the future by steering the cosmic flow. Our ability to envision what's next and to hold that vision while the details of its fulfillment show up, step by step by step, is crucial to navigating forward. To build this vision, we must know who we are and what is truly valuable. This applies both to our personal lives and our collective lives.

Personally, I believe that there are many souls on the planet who are here to help usher in this new era of sustainable, equitable, just, and abundant peace.

We are on the cusp of learning how to build this era.

But, right now, for many of us, it feels hard. And maybe it's a little frightening.

Many of us have been going through some of the motions necessary to create a better reality for ourselves and the world, but are not fully committing. We KNOW what we need to do, but we're not really doing it one hundred percent.

We're tired. We're confused. We feel like we're not seeing the results we hoped for. We feel like maybe we're doing it "wrong," and we don't have enough information to move forward. Misinformation and trying to figure out what's really going on is confusing. We're worried about what's next and how to prepare.

Maybe you relate?

All of this is normal. How you feel is normal. Even what's going on on the planet right now is normal.

(And it's not as bad as we are being made to believe by sensationalism and social media. In fact, statistics say the quality of life on our planet is better than it ever has been.)

But, we ARE at a crossroads.

Many of us are tired because we thought it would be easier. We thought we could simply show the world what else is possible, and the people around us would see how amazing the future looks, and they'd immediately join us.

So we took our message of growth, peace, and abundance out into the world, and people thought we were "dreamers," "unrealistic," "crazy," and maybe a bit "woo woo."

Our families looked at us funny. We lost friends. We outgrew some of our more intimate relationships. Making money and creating sustenance felt challenging and elusive.

And it was confusing.

Because you could FEEL in your Heart that what you understood was correct, but the world didn't seem to understand....

Here's the deal: When you are at a crossroads between system growth cycles, there is tension. Many people don't want to move forward and want to go back to the old ways when things felt more certain.

The forward momentum has to be tested and implemented and it doesn't always work right away. You have to tweak it and work with it, and because you've been so programmed to believe you have to get things "perfect" right away, you've mistakenly believed that you're failing.

You're not.

Two steps forward and one step back is still a step forward.

And perfection only comes with practice, and the journey to perfection is ALWAYS accompanied by trial and exploration.

I want to gently say that the tensions we are experiencing are symptoms of a system that is frantic about staying alive, but it won't. Evolution is inevitable.

But we do have a choice. We can either fight and resist our forward momentum, or we can trust the process and surrender. (This is the powerful message the planet Saturn is teaching us right now.)

Surrender DOES NOT MEAN QUITTING. In this case, surrender means that we need to put our heads down and keep doing the work.

Keep dreaming.

Keep envisioning.

Keep taking care of ourselves.

Keep clearing old limiting patterns and ancestral programming.

Keep deconditioning.

Keep doing the world that lights up your soul.

Keep. Moving. Forward.

And then take what you know out into the world. Not everyone will hear you, but the people who need what you have will be drawn to you.

One of my spiritual mentors is Buckminster Fuller. I want to leave you with one of my favorite "Bucky" quotes:

"You never change things by fighting the existing reality. To change something, build a new model that makes the existing model obsolete."

It is time for us to claim our right place and our right space in the world as leaders. In our evolving future, we will measure our wealth in terms of the quality of well-being we've cultivated. We will redefine our values and what is truly valuable.

We will build a world of equitable, just, sustainable, and abundant peace.

And it starts with you.

THIS is the work of 2025. We are tasked by the planets to keep our eyes on the future, to set a steady path forward as we fly through the storm of unpredictability.

As we begin the new year, let's start with an overview of the Nodes and the outer planets, which set the tone, lessons, and "plot outline" for the story of 2025.

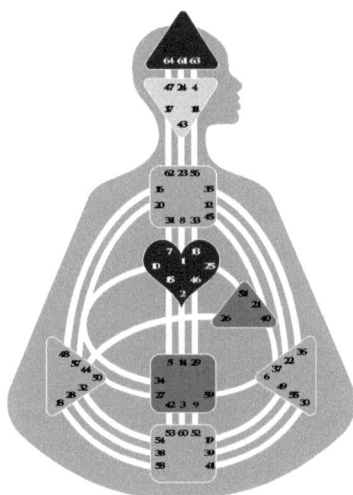

THE NODES:

The Nodes represent the "plot outline" in the story of the year ahead. The Nodal pairs reflect how we mature and evolve over the days ahead and what challenges we must overcome in order to fulfill the potential of this year.

Evolution is never linear. It's more like learning to ride a bike with training wheels. Much like we start with the training wheels close to the ground and raise them up until eventually removing them as the rider gets more comfortable with stabilizing the bike, evolution requires us to practice, learn new patterns, regulate our mindset, and then integrate new ways of being into our bodies as we grow.

This process of titrating our evolution is the theme of this year. We might feel wobbly, needing rest and time for practice and integration as we navigate our way forward. The Nodes give us a code for what we need to do to optimize our growth.

The Nodes this year include a deep theme of needing to "touch base" with our Higher Purpose, to be in communion with the Divine, and to remember to trust the process. We are invited to ignore the outer appearances and to stay internally aligned. We are breaking free from old patterns, both personal and ancestral. This work of liberating ourselves promises to challenge us mentally and physically, so the Nodes have kindly sprinkled in the need for rest and re-Sourcing so that we can sustain this deep process of untangling ourselves from our conditioning.

There is a secondary theme that plays out all year and needs to be heeded. We're at risk for burnout if we don't nurture ourselves in consistent and sustainable ways. We are being tasked with cultivating an inner AND outer self-generous environment. That means we may find ourselves setting hard boundaries and rewriting relationship contracts to preserve our own well-being and integrity.

Remember, you can't give to others until you have more than enough for yourself. We create more than enough when we heal our self-worth and know that we are inherently "enough" for whatever we are being called to do. Do not let self-doubt and doubt cause you to contract and hold yourself back from your own expansion.

The Nodes travel in pairs and lay out a mini-curriculum of learning, starting with the theme of the South Node, representing what needs to be mastered in order to move to the mature expression of the lesson in the North Node. The South Node represents what we need to learn to move forward, and the North Node represents the result of our growth.

JANUARY 1 - JANUARY 31

South Node: Gate 46 (The Gate of Embodiment)

North Node: Gate 25 (The Gate of Spirit)

We start the calendar year off with a gentle reminder to begin with a deep connection with your Higher Self and the purpose of your life. This reminder isn't about what you do, so much as it is about remembering who you are. You are a spiritual being born into a human story and the purpose of your life is to fulfill the unique role that only you can fulfill. The South Node lesson reminds us to check in with ourselves and make sure we're staying true to who we are.

The energy of both Nodal themes is rooted in the Heart of Who We Are. We are reminded to connect with Heart and take our direction in alignment with our authentic identity. If we do this, we embody our unique role in the world and sustain our vitality. Our bodies carry our spirits forward into action.

When we try to move in a direction that is misaligned with who we were born to be, our bodies eventually pay the price, disrupting our physical well-being in an attempt to get our attention and remind us to choose authentically without compromise.

JANUARY 31 - JUNE 13

South Node: Gate 6 (The Gate of Impact)

North Node: Gate 36 (The Gate of Exploration)

When the Nodes shift at the end of January, we move into the real work of the new Human Design year, which starts on January 21. The South Node theme highlights the need to disrupt old patterns. This is emotional work that asks you to think deeply about what you want and cultivate the faith to believe you can have it. This level of emotional alignment gives you the power to break free from patterns of the past.

In the shadow, Gate 36 brings chaos and distraction. When you struggle to hold your vision of the future and the ability to have faith that what you want is possible, you run the risk of losing focus and following the next "shiny object" that shows up and seems appealing. Boredom and frustration can lead to following creative potentials that lead nowhere and can rob you of energy. If you push too hard and out of alignment with right timing, you don't get the results you hope for, and things can fall apart in painful ways.

The North Node in the Gate 6 promises that we'll have reach and impact when we stay focused and faithful. The fulfillment of your vision not only brings the ability to truly impact others - including your loved ones - in a positive way, but also allows you to use your success to increase the success of others.

In the shadow, war, and scarcity live in Gate 6. If your dreams aren't coming true fast enough or if you've lost faith, it's easy to feel like a victim. This leads to a perspective of scarcity and feeling like you have to fight for your life and your resources. There's a tension here that can bleed over into relationships and cause deep emotional rifts. Tread carefully with your neighbors, and remember there is always more than enough. Tapping into abundance can only happen when you have faith that there is always more.

JUNE 13 - NOVEMBER 3

South Node: Gate 47 (The Gate of Mindset)

North Node: Gate 22 (The Gate of Surrender)

In the third Nodal configuration for the year, we again see the importance of mindset. Everything about the combination of these two Gates informs us that we are not in control of time and timing, but we can influence time and timing by trusting the process and making sure that our expectations and our faith line up. If we fail to trust that the answers we seek will appear when the timing is right, we default to our conditioned pattern of trying to "figure things out." We then run the risk of choosing options out of the same old box and being stuck in a pattern of frustration and, ultimately, an attitude of scarcity rather than expansiveness.

The highest expression of this combination of themes is the promise of clarity if we trust the process. We are instructed to let go, surrender, and hold the vibrational frequency we cultivate when we imagine the desired outcome. When we do this and cultivate our trust, we will be given all the resources we need to do what needs to be done.

This cycle reminds us that our dreams begin first on an energetic level. When we hold the energy and cultivate a practice that supports us, take some time during this cycle to cultivate a practice that brings you into harmony with your dreams. Take care of your mindset and be prepared for epiphanies that reveal to you your next right step.

NOVEMBER 3 - DECEMBER 23

South Node: Gate 64 (The Gate of Divine Transference)

North Node: Gate 63 (The Gate of Curiosity)

The Head Center and the Gates of the Head Center are the connections point between you and the Quantum Field of Infinite Possibilities. These interface energies invite us to not affirm or declare the answer, but to explore the options by asking for help and support and seeing what shows up in our outer reality or as inspiration. We are literally designed to pray through asking.

This transit encourages us to keep our eyes on the vision and dreams we seek to fulfill but to stay deeply in the question of who we need to be and what we need to do next to make our dreams come true. We are supported in engaging with the world through the lens of curiosity, awe, and wonder, to not "figure out" the answer to our questions but to stay engaged with our questions and explore the world like cosmic adventurers in quest of the right next steps to our fulfillment.

In the shadow, if we adopt a strictly materialistic view, these same two energies can inspire overwhelm, confusion, doubt and suspicion, not only towards the world, but within ourselves. If you have not grounded yourself in a practice of faith and answered with certainty the oh-so-important question of who you are, it is easy for this energy to feel destabilizing and heavy.

Give yourself lots of time to pray, explore, and cultivate a daily practice of staying inspired during this heavy energy.

Remember, all things begin first with inspiration.

DECEMBER 23

South Node: Gate 40 (The Gate of Restoration)

North Node: Gate 37 (The Gate of Peace)

We come to the end of our annual cycle with the Nodes bringing us somewhat full circle with our growth theme. Two steps forward, one step back is still one step forward. This "Cosmic Cha Cha Cha" is the nature of evolution in the human story. We progress. We surge forward, and then the story invites us to step back. It can feel like we're failing, but we are actually always in the process of aligning and making sure that our momentum is cleared of any vestiges of old limits and stories that need to be healed or released.

In this Nodal season, we're revisiting our relationships and our ancestral stories. We're looking at old agreements, both personal and collective, and ensuring they are still valid and fair. It's time to untangle ourselves from contracts that are no longer for our highest good. We're also strengthening the ties that bind and making new contracts reflecting our healed self-worth and sense of our true value.

This same energy can potentially bring up old relationship wounds and disappointment. This happens particularly if we entered into the relationship with hidden agendas or an expectation that our partner would "rescue" us from having to do the work of healing our ego. (Hint: No one can do that work for you.)

If you've overcommitted, built your relationships with mistaken motivations, sold yourself short, or denied your value, this is an important time to redefine the deals and even compromises you've made.

When we value ourselves, we forge strong bonds and make healthy agreements that are rooted in peace and sustainability. If we do the work of communicating clearly what we need and want, take good care of ourselves and each other, and we're authentic and aligned in our relationships and hold true to our value and values, this same energy allows us to deepen our connections, strengthen community, create resources and build a foundation for peace.

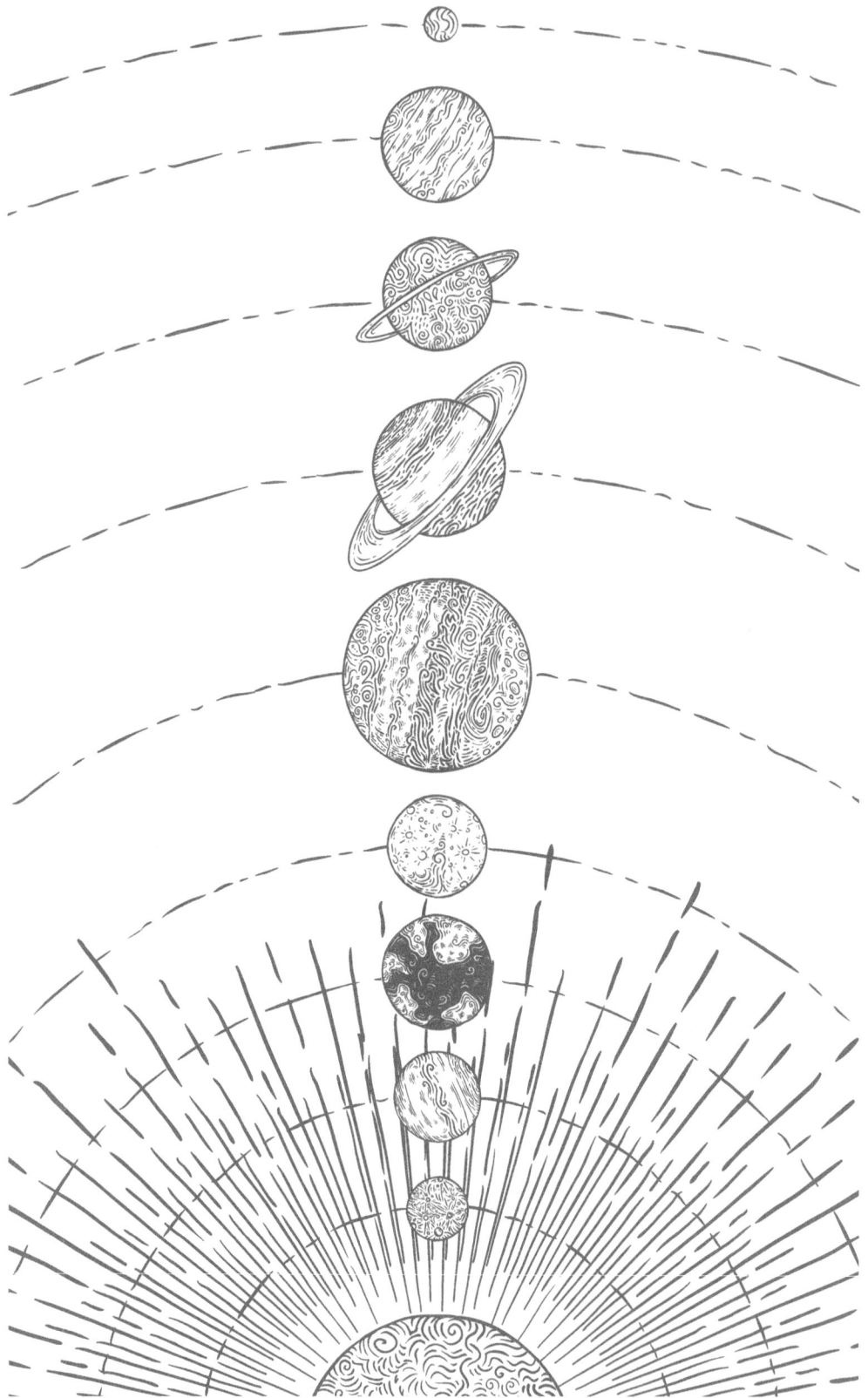

THE OUTER PLANETS

The outer planets, Uranus, Neptune, and Pluto, are creating quite the evolutionary matrix for massive change. They have been setting the stage for quantum leaps in human evolution since 2024 and will continue to do so until 2026.

One of the most important things that is happening with these slow-moving, collective planets is that all three are changing signs around the same time. At the same time, Neptune is also moving neck and neck with Saturn, adding more fuel to the evolutionary fire! As these planets surge forward, they are giving us a glimpse of what lies ahead before they all go retrograde towards the end of 2025. In 2026, these changes will stabilize, and we will see that we have passed through the last "dying gasp" of an old world and begun to lay a strong foundation for something better.

This huge shift in planetary weather has never happened before and sets us up for big changes in every part of the human story. I believe that as we pass through this threshold, we are heralding a new era of justice, equitability, sustainability, abundance, and peace. We will be learning to live in more communal and compassionate ways with greater integrity and accountability.

We are moving into an era where individuality matters, and our world is structured in such a way that individuality is not obliterated or negated by the needs of the collective. At the same time, we will also feel obligated (in a good way) to our communities, each one of us playing our unique, vital, and irreplaceable role. The aggregate effort of individuals will keep us going, and we will all understand that we only rise when we all rise together. This is the dawning of the Quantum Era and the emergence of the Quantum Human which you can read more about here: https://amzn. to/3tT3b0J

Some big themes that we'll see play out in the collective narrative include the contrast between narcissism and selfishness versus the ME within the WE. We will see the dissolution of facades, the embracing of the authentic and communities united around vibrational alignment.

This new era promises to be marked by even more rapid technological advances that will help us rewrite our human story. The children born starting in 2008 will be the creative leaders of this new era and promise to bring spiritual healing and innovation to the forefront.

The planets call on us to be strong and courageous, to self-regulate, to set healthy boundaries, to heal, to gauge our environment carefully, and to run from dogma.

Change is often met with resistance by those who are afraid of the unknown, but change does not equate to the need of the world, just the end of the world as we know it. This change is a new beginning with a lot of potential for goodness. Beware the purveyors of doom.

URANUS:

Gate 23 (Transmission) -> Gate 8 (Fulfillment) March 26 -> Gate 20 (Patience) July 10 -> Gate 8 (Fulfilment) November 5

Uranus, the "cosmic disruptor," brings the energy of the unexpected. Uranus loves to disrupt the status quo, bringing us unexpected shifts and changes that ultimately, force us to grow.

This year, Uranus begins its transition from Taurus to Gemini, moving into Gemini on July 7 before it returns for one last movement through Taurus on November 9. Uranus has been helping us dismantle old systems and breaking down circumstances and stories that are in need of rewriting and renegotiating. This dynamic planet in the Taurus position can be very uncomfortable and disruptive. Uranus tends to be more "comfortable" when highlighting the energy of Gemini.

This shift in Uranus signifies a movement away from the head and into a more expressive and creative energy. Over the course of its journey through Gemini, Uranus highlights the Gates of the Throat Center, helping us share, create, educate, and transmit new information. We are no longer taking things apart this year, we're using language to build the energetic template for something new and better.

But, we're not out of the woods. Uranus in Gemini has historically brought about the potential for war. We are at a crossroads in our evolution when the old materialistic and imperialist ideas are dying out, and we are embracing a deeper understanding of how borders and other-ing define natural law.

The quantum era initiates us into a deeper awareness that we are all unique expressions of a common field of energy. The challenges that face humanity will ultimately equalize us all as we begin to truly realize that we all live under the same sky and share the same planet.

NEPTUNE:

Gate 36 (Exploration -> Gate 25 (Spirit) February 10

This year, Neptune continues to promise us support in breaking free from the patterns of the past, provided that we root ourselves in a consistent and steady practice that supports us in cultivating faith.

Yes, faith is a practice. Most of us have to work to regain our natural faith. This takes consistency, a spiritual practice, a gratitude practice and doing the deep work of building and healing your self-worth. It's hard to sustain faith if you don't think you deserve to have what you desire.

When Neptune moves to Gate 25 in February, we refocus on our higher purpose - a contemplation that initiated us at the start of the calendar in the North Node. We're also healing any rifts in our relationship with Source so we can better allow ourselves to relax and trust, not only the process, but the timing of the unfolding.

PLUTO:

Gate 60 (Conservation) -> Gate 41 (Imagination) January 30 - > Gate 60 (Conservation) August 20 -> Gate 41 (Imagination) December 6

Pluto, the planet of death and rebirth, is wobbling at the end of the cosmic revolutionary cycle, delicately poised between - well - death and rebirth! The Gate 60 is the last Gate in the cycle of the Gates around the Human Design hexagram before we begin again on a new cycle around the wheel with the Gate 41.

Remember that evolution is not linear; it is more like titrating, drop by drop until we reach a critical mass for transformation. Pluto has been highlighting the Gate 60 for much of 2023 and, after spending a small bit of time highlighting the Gate 41, returned to the Gate 60 for most of last year. This year, we see this same cosmic dance playing out with Pluto and these two Gates.

Conservatism is an essential part of evolution. Evolution without checks and balances risks running wild without any way of knowing whether we're headed in the right direction. Mutation has to be experimented with and proven to be accurate and for the greatest good before we can trust our forward trajectory.

Forward movement is often hard-won. Some of us will fight to go back, and some of us will fight to move forward. The challenge is to find a path forward that honors and respects all perspectives. That means that all of humanity is charged with finding common ground as we move forward.

The secret sauce is not to fight or convince, but rather to put your head down, focus on what you want, build something amazing, and quietly show others how to do the same. One. Step. At. A. Time.

Patience and a willingness to play the long game are the keys to building a better world. Of course, as always, this means you must know who you are, what you want, and be clear on your value.

SATURN & JUPITER:

We finish up our overview of the major planetary movements by taking a closer look at Saturn and Jupiter. These two planets "dance" together in the sky, revealing the relationship between the work we must do and the rewards available to us when we do the work.

OVER THE COURSE OF THE YEAR, JUPITER HIGHLIGHTS THE FOLLOWING GATES:

January - Gate 35, The Gate of Experience

January 28 - Gate 16, The Gate of Zest

February 12 - Gate 35, The Gate of Experience

April 7 - Gate 45, the Gate of Distribution

May 7 - Gate 12, the Gate of the Channel

June 2 - Gate 15, the Gate of Compassion

June 27 - Gate 52, the Gate of Convergence

July 22 - Gate 39, the Gate of Re-Calibration

August 18 - Gate 53, the Gate of Starting

September 18 - Gate 62, the Gate of Preparation

January 6, 2026 - Gate 53. the Gate of Starting

SATURN HIGHLIGHTS THE FOLLOWING GATES:

January - Gate 63, the Gate of Curiosity

January 29 - Gate 22, the Gate of Surrender

March 17 - Gate 36, the Gate of Exploration

May 5 - Gate 25, the Gate of Spirit

September 25 - Gate 36, the Gate of Exploration

One important thing to pay attention to as we look at the lessons and blessings that Saturn and Jupiter bring us is that Saturn is also closely aligned with Neptune, bringing us a similar lesson but through the lens of Saturn, who is often considered the celestial taskmaster and a force that often removes obstacles out of our way if we get too distracted from the task at hand.

Saturn is also forcing us to take a closer look at our higher purpose and make sure we are not making excuses or letting distractions keep us from fulfilling the cosmic job we signed up for when we incarnated. This same energy offers us healing and the ability to disentangle ourselves from old patterns. Saturn promises to shackle us in place until we do the work and won't take "no" for an answer. If we resist, the only result will be burnout and a lot of wasted effort.

Jupiter highlights where we'll experience blessings and expansion if we do the work Saturn lays out for us. This year, Jupiter grants us the blessing of having greater impact and reach with our words, provided that we express our authentic selves. If we hide or obfuscate the truth, the payback from Saturn promises to be harsh. We can no longer lie to each other and to ourselves.

Once we hit June, Jupiter's theme shifts, and we are forced to focus on time, timing, and preparation to be ready for the next phase in our evolution and growth. We cannot control time and timing - a big lesson all around this year - but we can INFLUENCE it. Jupiter is encouraging us to take time to sit in silence, take a step back, and keep focused on the big picture.

We're also being reminded that time goes by faster when you have absolute faith. Doubt can gum up the wheels of time. We are also being reminded to finish up any unfinished business so we have room to start new things and, once we are internally aligned, to make sure we've taken the steps necessary to prepare the way on the physical plane. (In other words, build your website. Write your book. Do those things you've been holding yourself back from! Now is the time!)

2025 ECLIPSE SEASON

Eclipses serve as celestial checkpoints. An eclipse is a high-octane celestial event that helps illuminate our karmic path. Still, just as these cosmic events can be visually striking, eclipses can also be a bit dramatic. Astrologically speaking, eclipses speed up time. They open new doors by slamming others shut, so we often find abrupt and sudden shifts occurring during eclipses.

Though the shifts can be jarring, they can help us by speeding up the inevitable. So, if you've been dragging your feet, an eclipse will be sure to give you that extra push (or shove) needed to take action. While the results can be shocking, remember that these celestial events simply expedite the inevitable—these events were going to happen eventually.

Understanding transits helps you consciously harness the power of the transit and use it to your advantage. This won't necessarily help you avoid the intensity of these catalytic celestial events, but it will help you influence the outcome and better regulate your response to them. Remember, you can't always control what happens in your life, but you always have control over what you do with these events.

During solar eclipses, the Moon is directly between the Earth and the Sun, where the Sun and the Moon are said to be in conjunction. For some time, the tiny Moon has the capability to block out the giant Sun and turn off the lights on Earth. This might take away our perspectives in life. Solar eclipses are said to take away fixed patterns and push us into unknown realms.

Though this might cause upheavals in our lives, they are excellent growth promoters and powerful catalysts.

A lunar eclipse is an astronomical event that occurs when the Moon moves into the Earth's shadow, causing the Moon to be darkened. Astrologically, a lunar eclipse intensifies what needs to be brought to light in order for us to release, heal, align, or let go of limits that block us from fulfilling our goals and dreams. This energy delivers a powerful opening to growth by helping us explore what needs to be seen and revealed in order for us to create with greater integrity.

This year we finish the Aries/Libra axis themes with our last eclipse on the axis on March 29. The themes of the eclipse axis work hand in hand with the overarching astrological theme of the year, enhancing and deepening which aspects of our personal and collective stories we are evolving.

The Aries/Libra axis invites us into an inner dialogue that encourages us to be relentlessly authentic and even youthful or bold with our actions. Aries can be immature and headstrong, and they often need to be tempered by the quest for balance highlighted by Libra. Again, we are asking ourselves how we can be honest about who we are and what we need and diplomatic about how we can get our needs met. We are exploring our needs and wants, as well as any places where we perceive ourselves lacking. We are learning how to get these needs met in a sustainable, peaceful, and equitable way.

The Virgo/Pisces axis encourages us to explore how to shift a situation that feels unpleasant and stuck versus wallowing in our discontent. We are invited to look at which patterns need to be disrupted and re-ordered in order for us to create something new and better.

Below is a list of all the eclipse dates in this cycle, including the Human Design Gates highlighted with each eclipse.

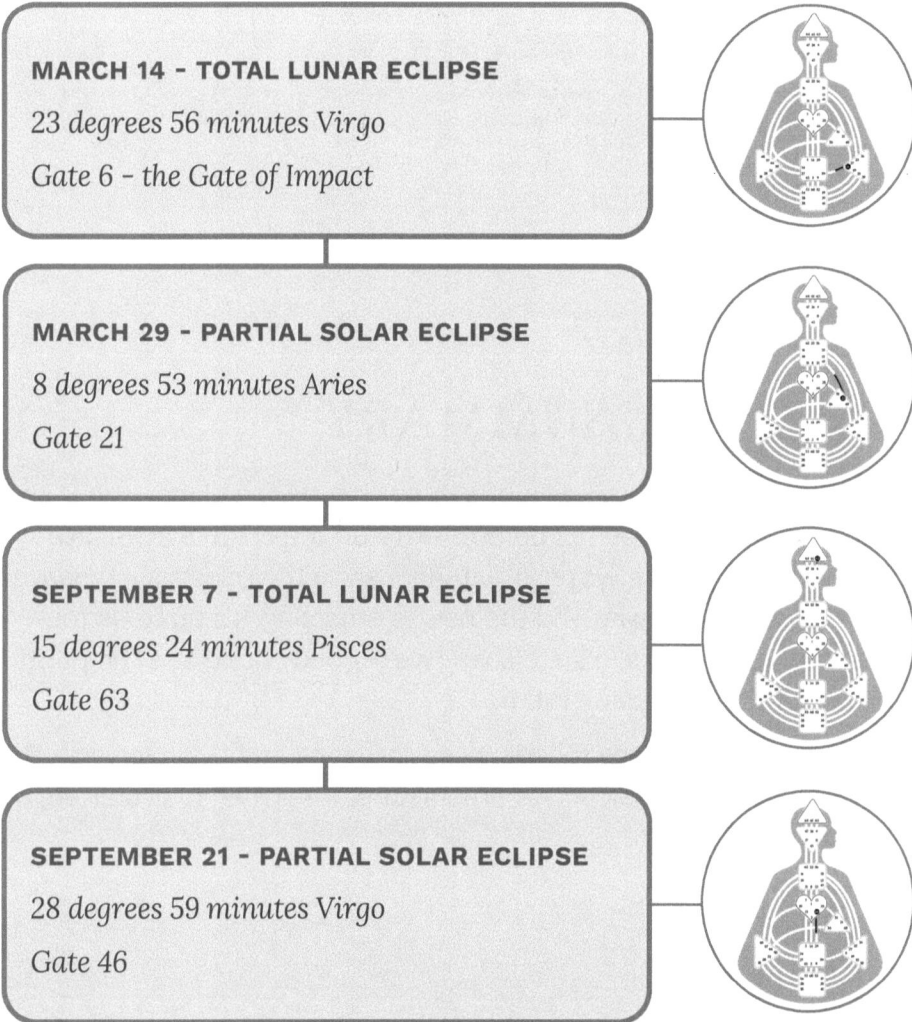

MARCH 14 - TOTAL LUNAR ECLIPSE

23 degrees 56 minutes Virgo

Gate 6 – the Gate of Impact

MARCH 29 - PARTIAL SOLAR ECLIPSE

8 degrees 53 minutes Aries

Gate 21

SEPTEMBER 7 - TOTAL LUNAR ECLIPSE

15 degrees 24 minutes Pisces

Gate 63

SEPTEMBER 21 - PARTIAL SOLAR ECLIPSE

28 degrees 59 minutes Virgo

Gate 46

The 2025 Evolution Guide contains special eclipse contemplations inserted on the dates of the 2025 eclipse events.

SUMMARY

We are right smack in the middle of a huge shift on the planet, the likes of which have never happened before. We're on the cusp of a creative revolution precisely while we're simultaneously in the midst of a creative crisis. The old is dying away, and the new is emerging. It's up to us to engineer our way forward in such a way we embody hope and the promise of an abundant and peaceful future.

Take care of yourselves, my friends. Keep adjusting and flying towards the horizon. One day, we'll look at this time as the time when it all started, and it was good.

From my Heart to Yours,

Karen

EVOLUTION GUIDE

MY CHART

Using this information and your own chart, which you can get at **www.freehumandesignchart.com,** have fun coloring in your Defined Gates and Centers on the chart below:

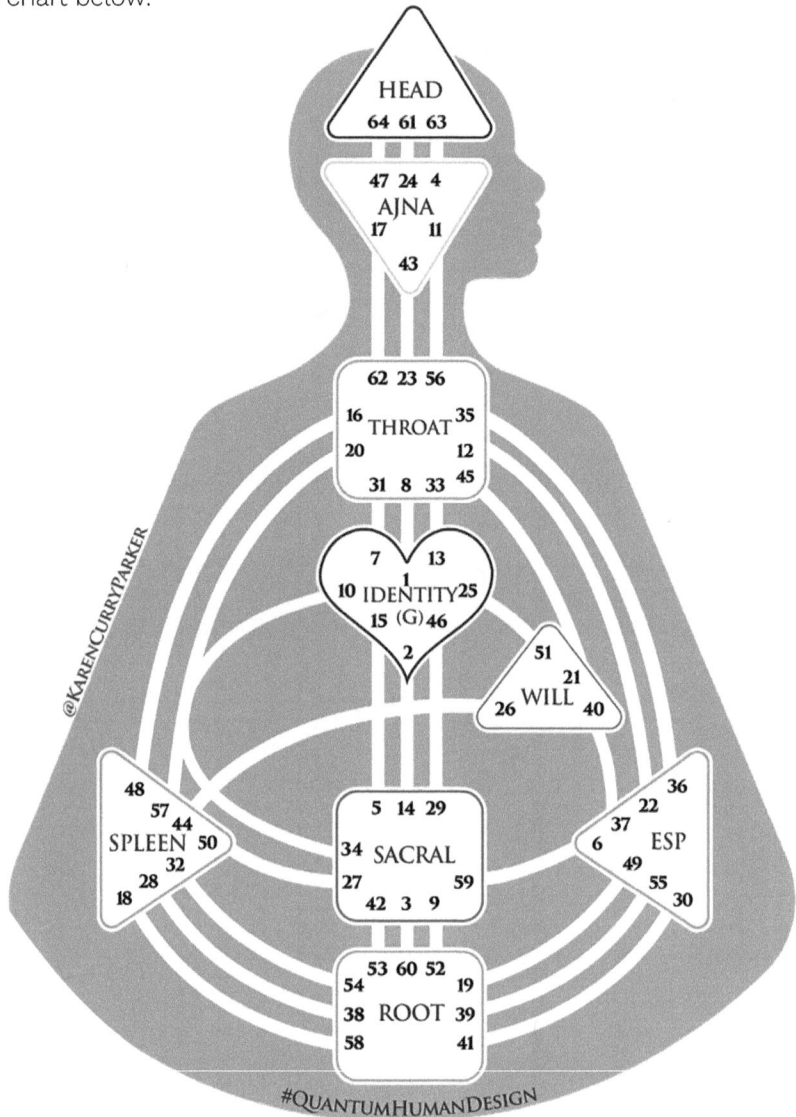

HEAD
64 61 63

47 24 4
AJNA
17   11
43

62 23 56
16 **THROAT** 35
20   12
31 8 33 45

7   13
1
10 IDENTITY 25
15 (G) 46
2

51
21
26 WILL 40

48
57   36
44   22
SPLEEN 50   37
32   6   **ESP**
28   49
18   55
30

5 14 29
34 **SACRAL**
27   59
42 3 9

53 60 52
54   19
38 **ROOT** 39
58   41

@KarenCurryParker

#QuantumHumanDesign

32

MY CHART HIGHLIGHTS

My Type _____

My Profile _____

My Defined Centers _____

My Open Centers _____

My Conscious Sun _____

My Unconscious Sun _____

My Conscious Earth _____

My Unconscious Earth _____

Traditional HD	Quantum HD	Shadow Aspect	High Expression
Types			
Manifestor	Initiator	Powerlessness / Power Struggles	Deeply connected to Divine Inspiration and the flow of Spirit. Deep connection to the value of the role that only an Initiator can play. Own their own power, knows when to inform and move forward when the timing is right. Serves as a creative muse and a transformational agent of change.
Generator	Alchemist	Quitting through frustration / Trying to figure out what's next	Explore through responding, enduring, sustaining, practice, repetition and correction to learn who they are and how they respond to life. Cultivates a deep and aligned relationship to their purpose and path and trust that the next level will be revealed when they are ready.
Manifesting Generator	Time Bender	Quitting through frustration / anger / disruption	Aware of their power and speed. Deeply conscious of those around them who will be impacted by their fast response to life. They are tuned in to their Sacral Centre to wait to respond. In alignment gives creative flow that brings change, transformation and creativity. Their ability to 'do' transforms people perceptions of what is possible
Projector	Orchestrator	Feeling unheard and unseen / burnout	Nurtures and cares for their mind, body and spirit with great deliberation. Understands that timing and waiting work in their favour by resting between activations to restore their energy. They know their value and will share with the right people at the right time. Trust right timing. Here to manage, guide and delegate to conserve their energy
Reflector	Calibrator	Trying to fix others / feeling exhausted and disappointed with the World	Aware of their surroundings and the experience of their surroundings within them. Feel in alignment with their community. Feel like they are 'home' with the people and the environment around them. Takes the time to be in alignment with what is right for them. They are a reflection and need to 'be' with it and it's not their job to fix it.

Traditional HD	Quantum HD	Shadow Aspect	High Expression
Lines			
1 Investigator	Resource	Fear of not knowing enough / fear of the unknown	To lay the information foundation for the security and safety of all of us. To value and trust your curiosity. Celebrate and value the depth of your knowledge
2 Hermit	Responder	Fear of disappearing and being isolated	To integrate knowledge, energy and wisdom, and wait for the readiness of others to call them out. Needs alone time to rest, integrate and regenerate so that you're ready when it's time to share what you know.
3 Martyr	Explorer	Fear of Failure	To explore and experience possibilities and share your experiences with others to protect and serve them. Needs to experiment and try things to gain Mastery to share insights with others.
4 Opportunist	Stabilizer	Fear of loss or being in limbo	To lay the foundation of community and connection and prepare the way for sharing and spreading of ideas. To learn how to facilitate change and be in the flow and to use this knowledge to help others. To bring stability to the community with your wisdom
5 Heretic	Visionary Leader	Fear of not being truly seen or heard / Being subject to false expectation of others	To serve as a "Karmic Mirror" for others and to support the healing process through the reflection by teaching and sharing the highest potential of humanity possible. To teach, lead and inspire those who are ready and to be able to gauge who you are here to lead.
6 Role Model	Adept	Fear of failing your Life Purpose	To experience, integrate and demonstrate the highest potential of consciousness on the planet and to quietly show us how to live it. Phase 1 to fearlessly experiment and explore to discover what works best. Phase 2 To integrate what you've learned and to rest, heal, learn and explore your own creative plane. Phase 3 To live as the ruler of aligned and authentic living - show the world by walking your talk.

Traditional HD	Quantum HD	Shadow Aspect	High Expression
Centers			
Head	Quantum Interface	**Defined:** Feeling uninspired	**Defined:** A conduit for inspiration. To use inspiration with responsibility and awareness. To recognize your role as an inspirational force in the world.
		Open: Confusion, lost, pressure, self doubt	**Open:** To be the observer of inspiration. To trust that the inspirations that are yours to follow will reveal themselves on the material plane.
Ajna	Divine Translator	**Defined:** Closed minded, locked in negative thought patterns	**Defined:** To generate expansive ideas and concepts and envision them until the details of how to materialize these ideas reveal themselves.
		Open: Under pressure to figure things out, fear of the unknown, trying to hold a fixed vision	**Open:** To see ideas from many different perspectives and to be open minded on how you envision and imagine. To embrace unlimited possibilities and make peace with the unknown.
Throat	Activation	**Defined:** Speaking without what for right timing, using words irresponsibly	**Defined:** To wait for the right cues and clues to know how to share information or words that elevate and increase potential.
		Open: Feel pressure to speak, trying to prove your value, not waiting for right timing or right people	**Open:** To learn to trust the Divine flow of information. To trust when the timing and the environment is correct, you'll be able to share what you know with words that best meet the needs of others.
Identity (G)	Calibration	**Defined:** Afraid you won't be loved for expressing your Authentic Self	**Defined:** To recognize that you are designed to love, to be empowered, to control your own personal narrative, to use your life in service to your Higher Self, to stay vital, to explore how much goodness you're willing to allow and to share it compassionately with the world. To trust that when you express your Authentic Self, you are moving in a direction that supports your sustainability and abundance and energetically shows the way to others.
		Open: Questioning your lovability, struggle with direction	**Open:** To be deeply wise about the potential of the story of humanity. To choose which elements of the human condition and narrative you want to integrate as part of yourself. To know who you are is evolving and expanding. To use other people's narratives to consciously calibrate your own direction.

Traditional HD	Quantum HD	Shadow Aspect	High Expression
Will	Resource	**Defined:** To push and use force of Will, low self worth, to aversive and deplete self, burnout	**Defined:** To give from abundant resources and stay consistently resourced to avoid cycles of depletion and exhaustion. To live and create from a place of knowing your value and taking right actions to take up your right place and right space. To live and create in physical, resource, identity, moral and energetic integrity. To use conscious rest and re-Sourcing yourself as a way of sustaining integrity. Knowing who you are serves as a unique and vital role in serving others.
		Open: Taking actions and choice to prove your value to others	**Open:** To evaluate integrity and alignment with value in others. To gauge your level of investment in circumstances that do not match your own value and values. To have the freedom to consciously choose what you considerate be valuable and build you life around it. To live from an internal sense of your own value. To learn to trust in sufficiency. To fully embody 'enoughness'. (I AM enough....)
Emotional Solar Plexus	Creative	**Defined:** Making emotional decisions in the moment, feeling disappointment, anger, frustration or bitterness	**Defined:** To know how to envision a deliberate outcome and wait to endure the desire for the outcome stays consistent no matter how your mood may fluctuate.
		Open: Give up what you need to be happy, compromise on your dreams, values for others	**Open:** To hold your emotionally frequency even when others struggle to sustain theirs.
Sacral	Evolution	**Defined:** Pushing too hard, compromising on your inner Wisdom, quitting before you self actualize	**Defined:** To trust your inner alignment and innate responding nature to allow the unfolding of Life's Intelligent plan of action through you.
		Open: To not know when enough is enough, burn out by overdoing it	**Open:** To experience life force energy and vitality and use it to guide and direct others to do the work. To know what needs to be done and to tap into resources to facilitate getting it done without actually having to do it yourself.

Traditional HD	Quantum HD	Shadow Aspect	High Expression
Spleen	Self-Actualization	**Defined:** Hypervigilant, avoidance or over-preparing driven by fear so not getting things done	**Defined:** The presence and awareness to know what you need to know when you need to know it and do what you need to do when you need to do it to be aligned with sustainability, integrity and expansion.
		Open: Holding onto things/ people/ situations longer than is healthy. Preparing for worst case	**Open:** To feel the alignment with courage in to the room and to uplift others. To overcome fear and find presence and be centered.
Root	Divine Timing	**Defined:** Not waiting for right timing, burnout, not being ready when the time aligned	**Defined:** To be deeply connected to the accompanying energy flow state this experienced when the timing for action is aligned.
		Open: Feeling pressured, stressed, not trusting right timing, burnout	**Open:** To use adrenaline energy in a sustainable way to ensure right action at the right time.
Circuits & Subcircuits			
Individual	Transformation	To rebel in reaction to feeling uncertain and insecure. To ignore right timing and readiness and share what you know without waiting. To feel hurt, left out and the need to compromise who you are to feel loved and accepted. To not honor the transformation you have to bring enough to value yourself and your unique contribution to the world.	The ability to stay true to your authentic identity with the awareness that you fulfilling the full expression of your identity and inspiration creates the potential of a wave of new possibility for humanity. To serve as a global change agent by simply being the fullest expression of yourself. To know that your authentic story transforms the world.

Traditional HD	Quantum HD	Shadow Aspect	High Expression
Individual • Integration	Transformation • Unifying	To be reactive, depleted from pushing against right timing and failing to fulfill potential due to lack of self-love and self-trust.	The ability to be responsively powerful in alignment with inner and outer timing and Love while serving the fulfillment of the full potential of the human condition.
Individual • Centering	Transformation • Calibration *(aura-busting)*	To blindly follow your own path without respect to how it impacts others. To take actions that overcompensate for a sense of lack of lovability, low self-worth, a disconnection from Purpose and Heart and a distrust of Source/God.	The ability to embody a deep relationship and trust of Source, Higher Self and the fulfillment of Purpose in order to lead others by demonstrating "The Way". To initiate others into following their own Hearts by showing the world what it looks like to live form Heart.
Individual • Knowing	Transformation • Gnostic	To share what you know before people are ready. To feel outcast, strange or alienated because people aren't ready for what you know. To exhaust yourself pushing your knowingness at the wrong time or with the wrong people.	The ability to trust in what you know you know and to trust that you'll know what you need to know when you need to know it. The ability to trust in your purpose as a transformational agent on the planet and to let timing and circumstances inform you about when you need to share what you know. To sow the seeds of change with your knowledge and to transform the way people think, create and connect to Source.

Traditional HD	Quantum HD	Shadow Aspect	High Expression
Tribal	Sustainability	The fear of not having enough creates hoarding, hiding, stealing and war. The refusal to share out of fear of lack. Selfish actions or martyrdom. Depletion, exhaustion and burnout that creates tension and projection. Compromising what you really want for the sake of others and feeling resentful and exhausted. The failure to take care of yourself so that you have more to give.	The ability to create sustainable resources and share them with others. The mastery of sharing and the embodiment of love as a verb. The ability to create peaceful agreements that are rooted in the possibility of win-win negotiation and justice. The management of resources that allows you to share what you have from a place of sufficiency. The ability to respond to the needs of others in a sustainable, peaceful and just way.
Tribal • Defense	Sustainability · Nurture *(aura-busting)*	Co-Dependency, over-caring, assuming responsibility for things you're not responsible for and making impulsive, defensive choices that can lead to war and destruction.	The ability to respond to the need to do the work necessary to nurture and sustain resources. To educate for the sake of cultivating the right values that are rooted in nurturing, sustainable choices. Builds the foundation of love in action.
Tribal • Ego	Sustainability • Economic	Letting fear and lack create overwhelm and misuse of power and resources.	The ability to respond to the right need at the right time to create sustainable value and shared resources.
Collective	Synergy	Rigidly adhering to old patterns or unproven ideas and trying to construct false systems with inaccurate information or rigidly adhering to old systems and stories that are not supported by truth.	The ability to understand past experiences and patterns and to use these understandings to built collective infrastructures and systems that allow us to fully express our humanity and to ensure the survival of the species.

Traditional HD	Quantum HD	Shadow Aspect	High Expression
Collective • Logic/ Understanding	Synergy • Pattern	To adhere so rigidly to patterns that you miss the pattern interrupt. Letting fear, doubt and suspicion keep you from changing the pattern. Discounting the wisdom of the Heart.	The ability to test and experiment with information in order to understand patterns. The use of patterns to predict future outcomes.
Collective • Sensing	Synergy • Miracle	To allow ungrounded fantasy and old painful experiences from the past set the tone and the direction for life. Chaos or rigidity.	The ability to use the power of story telling and personal narrative to break old patterns and to expand the story of what is possible.

Gate	Traditional HD Gate Name	Quantum HD Gate Name	Shadow Aspect	High Expression
1	Self-Expression	Purpose	An erratic or purposeless life, panic, anxiety due to a feeling of 'failing' at a life 'mission', pressure to create something unique in the world, struggle to find purpose, hiding out because the purpose feels 'too big', too much or egotistical.	The ability to know the Authentic Self and a deep connection with a Life Purpose.
2	Keeper of the Keys	Allowing	To experience stress, fear and ultimately compromise on what you want and who you are because you don't trust that you're supported. To be valiantly self- sufficient to the point of burning yourself out. To never ask for help.	To set intentions and move solidly towards the fulfillment of the Authentic Self with complete trust that you are supported in being the full expression of who you are and your life purpose, even if you don't know how or what the support will look like. Trust in Source. Living in a state of gratitude.
3	Ordering	Innovation	To feel pressured and panicked to share an idea or innovation. To burn yourself out trying to override Divine Timing.	The ability to embrace and integrate new ideas and new ways of doing things. To learn to stay in appreciation for your unique way of thinking and being and to trust that, as an innovator on the leading edge of consciousness, your time to transmit what you're here to bring forth will come, so you wait and cultivate your ideas with patience.
4	Answers	Possiblity	Self-doubt and fear that you have an idea that you can't figure out. The pressure to try to share or implement the idea before it has had time to "seed" the manifestation. Acting too soon without waiting for the right timing.	The ability to experience an idea as a possibility, to learn to use the idea as a "seed" for the imagination and to use the imagination to create an emotional response which then calibrates the Heart and attracts experiences and opportunities that match the possibility into your life.

Gate	Traditional HD Gate Name	Quantum HD Gate Name	Shadow Aspect	High Expression
5	Patterns	Consistency	Life will seem like a constant struggle to stay connected and live habitually in a way that creates stability, sustainability and a fulfilled expression.	The ability to stay consistent with habits and choices that bring you closer to living true to who you are through alignment, and not overusing will power.
6	Friction	Impact	Feeling desperate, emotionally reactive, lacking, invisible, and being willing to do whatever it takes to take resources and energy for your own good, irregardless of the means. Fear that you'll never be seen or heard.	Maintaining a high frequency of emotional energy that supports equitability, sustainability and peace. Using your emotional alignment to influence others and to serve as an energetic beacon of peace and sufficiency.
7	Self in Interaction	Collaboration	To struggle and fight to be seen and recognized as the leader at cost to your energy and the fulfillment of your purpose..	To embrace that power comes from supporting, influencing and collaborating with leadership. To recognize that you don't have to be the figurehead to influence the direction that leadership assumes. The chief of staff is often more powerful than the president. The energy to unify people around an idea that influences the direction of leadership.
8	Contribution	Fulfillment	Feeling panicked and disconnected from your Life Purpose. Thinking that your Life Purpose is something you have to "do" versus someone you have to "be". To try to be someone you're not in an attempt to serve as a "role model".	To push the edges and boundaries of authentic self-expression and to realize that you being the full expression of your authentic self IS your life purpose. To use your authentic expression to inspire others to fulfill themselves.
9	Focus	Convergence	Feeling pressured to figure out where to place your focus. Feeling overwhelmed and confused by too many options and choices. Not being able to see the relationship between ideas and actions and missing the important details.	The ability to see the "big picture" and be able to prioritize where to focus your energy.

Gate	Traditional HD Gate Name	Quantum HD Gate Name	Shadow Aspect	High Expression
10	Love of Self	Self-Love	To question your lovability, struggle to prove your love-worthiness, to give up and settle for less than what you deserve and to blame others for your circumstances and situations. Victim consciousness.	To see your love for yourself as the source of your true creative power.
11	Ideas	The Conceptualist	Desperately trying to force every idea you have into manifestation.	The awareness that you are a vessel for ideas. To understand that those ideas are for you to hold and protect until the right person comes along for you to share them with. To relax as the vessel and know that not all ideas are yours to build upon. To use the power of your inspiration to stimulate the imagination of yourself and others.
12	Caution	The Channel	The struggle to try to speak ideas into form when it's not the right time. Letting hesitancy and caution paralyze you. Trying to force ideas and words.	To know that your voice is an expression of transformation and a vehicle for Divine Insight. The words you speak, the insights and creativity you share have the power to change others and the world. This energy is so powerful that people have to be ready to receive it. When you are articulate, then the timing is correct. If you struggle to find the words, have the courage to wait until it feels more aligned. A powerful ability to craft language and creative expressions that changes people's perceptions.
13	The Listener	Narrative	Staying stuck in old stories. Holding on to old past pains. Staying the victim in a story that repeats itself because your personal narrative is stuck in an old story.	The ability to use the power of personal narrative to create with power and intention.

Gate	Traditional HD Gate Name	Quantum HD Gate Name	Shadow Aspect	High Expression
14	Power Skills	Creation	Fear and worry about money. Being willing to compromise your "right" work to do whatever you have to do for material gain.	The ability to be at peace about having resources. To be in a constant state of trust that everything you need will show up in your outer reality in accordance with your alignment with Source. The resources you have allow you to increase the resources for others. To change the definition of "work". To no longer work for material gain, but work for the sake of transforming the world and being in the flow of life. To know that support flows from alignment with your Heart.
15	Extremes	Compassion	Self-judgement and extreme habits that are frenetic and non-productive. Trying to force your natural waves of rhythm into the daily practices and habits that society defines as "successful" and struggling with follow-through. Denying your own Heart. Being too afraid to do what feels right.	The ability to trust your own flow and rhythm, to trust that you will have cycles that disrupt old patterns and force you to re-create your direction and flow. To learn to set parameters for your creativity and work within the parameters when it feels right and then rest in between. Nature has rhythm AND extremes. You are here to change old rhythms and patterns to align them with greater compassion.
16	Skills	Zest	Having a pattern of leaping into the unknown without sufficient preparation. Not assessing whether an idea or inspiration is actually an expression of mastery. "Leaping without looking." Holding yourself back when you know the time is right because others tell you you're "not ready".	The courage to trust your own intuition that the timing is right and you are "ready enough" even if you don't know exactly how your journey will unfold. Faith in the outcome.

Gate	Traditional HD Gate Name	Quantum HD Gate Name	Shadow Aspect	High Expression
17	Opinions	Anticipation	To share opinions that degrade options. To embrace opinions as truth and act on them. To create personal and collective narratives that are negative and filled with doubt.	To use the power of your mind to explore potentials and possibilities that stretch our ideas about what else is possible in the human condition. To use your thoughts to inspire others to think bigger and bolder. To use your words to inspire and set the stage for creating energy that expands potential.
18	Correction	Re-Alignment	To be critical. To share criticism without respect for the impact. To be more concerned with your own "rightness" than to assess whether your insight is actually adding to more joy in the world.	To see a pattern that needs correcting and to wait for the right timing and circumstances to correct and align it. To serve joy.
19	Wanting	Attunement	Being overly sensitive and shutting down or compromising your own needs and wants. Feeling disconnected from others as a way of coping with being overly sensitive. Being emotionally clingy or needy as a way of forcing your natural desire for intimacy.	The ability to sense the emotional needs of others and your community, and know how to bring the emotional energy back into alignment with sufficiency and sustainability. The ability to be emotionally vulnerable and present to increase Heart to Heart connections.
20	Metamorphosis	Patience	To act before the time is right. To fail to listen to your inner guidance and prepare. To feel pressure to take action before the time is right and to feel frustrated or to quit.	The ability to trust your intuition, to know what needs to be set in place, what people need to be gathered, what skills need to be mastered and to be ready when the time is right. To trust in the right timing and to heed the intuition to get ready.

Gate	Traditional HD Gate Name	Quantum HD Gate Name	Shadow Aspect	High Expression
21	The Treasurer	Self-Regulation	To feel the need to control life, others, resources, etc. out of fear that you aren't worthy of being supported.	The ability to regulate your inner and outer environment in order to sustain a vibrational frequency that reflects your true value. The ability to be self-generous and to set boundaries that maintain your value and support you in being sustainable in the world. To take the actions necessary to honor your unique role in the cosmic plan.
22	Openness	Surrender	Fear that you are not supported. Holding back or stifling your passion because you think you can't "afford" to pursue it. Compromising, settling or letting despair regulate your emotional energy, causing the creative process to feel shut down or stuck.	The grace to know that you are fully supported by the Universal flow of abundance and to pursue your passion and your unique contribution to the world no matter what. To trust that you will be given what you need when you need it in order to make your unique contribution to the world.
23	Assimilation	Transmission	The need to be right. An anxiety or pressure to share what you know with people who aren't ready and then to feel despair or bitterness that they don't understand things the way that you do.	The ability to be able to translate transformative insights for people that offer them a way to transform the way they think. To share what you know with awareness of right timing, and to trust your knowingness as an expression of your connection to Source.
24	Rationalization	Blessings	To protect yourself by staying stuck in old patterns. To refuse to transform. To rationalize allowing less than what you deserve.	To recognize all experiences have the potential for growth and expansion. To redefine the stories of your experiences to reflect what you learned and how you grew. To be grateful for all of your life experiences and to liberate yourself from stories that no longer serve you.

Gate	Traditional HD Gate Name	Quantum HD Gate Name	Shadow Aspect	High Expression
25	Love of Spirit	Spirit	Fear and mistrust of Spirit. Using your life strictly for personal gains regardless of the impact on others. Ego in the lowest expression. Not feeling worthy of being loved by Source and using your willpower to create instead of alignment.	To connect with Source with consistency and diligence so as to fulfill your Divine Purpose and fulfill the true story of who you are and the role you play in the Cosmic Plan. To use your alignment with Source as a way of healing the world.
26	The Trickster	Integrity	To learn to value your right place and your value enough to act as if you are precious. To heal past traumas and elevate your self-worth. To trust in divine support enough to do the right thing, and to nurture yourself so that you have more to give.	To live in moral, energetic, identity, physical and resource integrity with courage and trust. To set clear boundaries and take the actions necessary to preserve the integrity of your right place.
27	Responsibility	Accountability	Co-dependency. Guilt (feels guilty or makes others feel guilty) Over-caring. Martyrdom.	The ability to support, nurture and lift others up. To sense and to act on what is necessary to increase the wellbeing of others and the world. To "feed" people with healthy food and healthy nourishment to ensure that they thrive. To hold others accountable for their own self-love and self-empowerment.
28	Struggle	Adventure/ Challenge	Refusing to take action out of fear that the journey will be too painful, wrought with struggle, or that you will fail. To feel like a failure. To fall into victim consciousness.	To learn to share from your personal experience, your struggles and your triumphs. To persevere and to know that the adventures in your life deepen your ability to transform life into a meaningful journey. To understand that your struggles help deepen the collective ideas about what is truly valuable and worthy of creating.

Gate	Traditional HD Gate Name	Quantum HD Gate Name	Shadow Aspect	High Expression
29	Perseverance	Devotion	To over-commit. To not know when to let go and when enough is enough. To fail to commit to the right thing. To burn out and deplete yourself because you don't say "yes" to yourself. To do something just because you can, not because you want to.	The ability to respond to committing to the right thing. To know that your perseverance and determination changes the narrative of the world and shows people what is possible. Your devotion sets the tone for the direction that life takes you.
30	Desire	Passion	Burnout. Impatience and not waiting for the right timing. Misdirected passion that is perceived as too much intensity. Leaping into chaos.	The ability to sustain a dream, intention and a vision until you bring it into form. To inspire others with the power of your dream. To inspire passion in others.
31	Democracy	The Leader	To push and seize leadership for the sake of personal gain, or to be afraid to lead and not feel worthy of serving as a leader.	The ability to be able to listen, learn, hear and serve the people you lead and to assume and value your right leadership position as the voice for the people you are leading.
32	Continuity	Endurance	Letting the fear of failure cause you to avoid preparing what you need to do. To not be ready when the timing is right. To push too hard, too fast, and too long against right timing.	The awareness of what needs to be done in order to make a dream manifested reality. Setting the stage, preparation, being ready. The patience and trust that once the stage is set, the timing will unfold as needed to serve the highest good of all. To translate Divine inspiration into readiness.
33	Privacy	Retelling	Staying stuck and sharing a personal narrative rooted in pain, disempowerment and victimhood.	The ability to translate a personal experience into an empowering narrative that teaches and gives direction to others. Finding the power from the pain. Waiting for the right timing to transform or share a narrative so that it has the greatest impact on the Heart of another.

Gate	Traditional HD Gate Name	Quantum HD Gate Name	Shadow Aspect	High Expression
34	Power	Power	Being too busy to tune into the right timing and the right people. Feeling frustrated with pushing and "trying" to make things happen. Forcing manifestation with little results. Depleting yourself because you're pushing too hard.	The ability to respond to opportunities to unify the right people around a transformative and powerful idea when the timing and circumstances are correct.
35	Change	Experience	To be bored with life. To let the boredom of life cause you to settle for a life that never challenges the status quo.	The ability to know which experiences are worthy and worthwhile. To partake in the right experience and to share your knowledge from the experience for the sake of changing the story of what's possible in the world.
36	Crisis	Exploration	Not waiting for the right timing and leaping into new opportunities without waiting for alignment, causing chaos. To leap from opportunity to opportunity without waiting to see how the story will play out and never getting to experience the full fruition of the experience.	The ability to hold a vision and sustain it with an aligned frequency of emotional energy and to bring the vision into form when the timing is right. The ability to stretch the boundaries of the story of Humanity by breaking patterns. Creating miracles through emotional alignment.
37	Friendship	Peace	Desperately struggling to find peace outside of yourself. Trying to control the outer world to create inner peace.	The ability to stay connected to sustainable peace and to respond to life by generating peace no matter what is happening in your external reality. Creating the emotional alignment to make peaceful choices no matter what's going on in the outer world.
38	The Fighter	The Visionary	To struggle and fight for the sake of fighting. Engaging in meaningless fights. Aggression and struggle.	The ability to know what's worth committing to and fighting for. To use your experiences to craft a vision that anchors the possibility of something truly meaningful and worthy in the world. Serving the world as a visionary.

Gate	Traditional HD Gate Name	Quantum HD Gate Name	Shadow Aspect	High Expression
39	Provocation	Recalibration	Feeling overwhelmed by lack and panicking. Hoarding, over-shopping as a result of fear of lack. Provoking and challenging others and holding others responsible for your own inner alignment with sufficiency.	The ability to transform an experience into an opportunity to shift to greater abundance. To see and experience internal or external lack and to use your awareness of lack to re-calibrate your energy towards sufficiency and abundance.
40	Loneliness	Restoration	Martyrdom. Loneliness and blaming that causes you to compromise what you need and try to prove your value by overdoing and over-giving.	The ability to retreat as a way of replenishing your inner and outer resources and to bring your renewed Self back into community when you are ready so that you have more to give.
41	Fantasy	Imagination	To imagine worst-case scenarios and fixate on them. Denying your creative capacity and abdicating your creative power. Being afraid to share other options because they defy the current expectations or patterns. Being afraid of being judged by others for being a "dreamer".	The ability to use your creative imagination to generate ideas about new abundant opportunities in the world. To sustain these abundant visions, share them when necessary, and use your imagination to break old patterns and limiting beliefs. To be able to hold the vision of a miracle that transcends expectations.
42	Finishing Things	Conclusion	Pressure, confusion, self-judgement for not being able to 'get things started'. Avoiding or putting off things that need to be completed creating a backlog of projects that can lead to paralysis and overwhelm. Finishing things prematurely due to pressure.	The ability to respond to being put into opportunities, experiences and events that you have the wisdom to facilitate and complete. To know exactly what needs to be completed in order to create the space for something new.

Gate	Traditional HD Gate Name	Quantum HD Gate Name	Shadow Aspect	High Expression
43	Insight	Insight	Feeling despair or frustration related to having knowledge, but struggling to share what you know. Experiencing lightning bolts of knowingness and clarity, but feeling overwhelmed by your inability to articulate what you understand. Not waiting for the right time to share what you know and feeling alone with your wisdom.	The ability to tap into new knowledge, understandings and insights that expand people's understanding of the world. To align with the right timing and trust that you'll know how to share what you know when you need to share it.
44	Energy	Truth	Fear and paralysis that the patterns of the past are insurmountable and doomed to repeat themselves.	The ability to see patterns that have created pain. To bring awareness to help yourself and others break old patterns and transform pain into an increased sense of value and alignment with purpose.
45	The King or Queen	Distribution	Diva energy. Selfish leadership that is rooted in lack and showing off. Holding back. Overcompensating for a lack of self-worth with narcissism. Fear of not being seen as a leader and reacting by being controlling or pompous and egotistical or bombastic.	The ability to understand that knowledge and material resources are powerful, and to know how to use both as a path of service that sustains others and helps others grow their own abundant foundation.
46	Love of Body	Embodiment	To disconnect from the body. To hate the body. To avoid nurturing or taking care of the body. To avoid the commitments and consistency necessary to fully embody life force. To hide or disfigure the body.	To recognize that the body is the vehicle for the soul and to love the body as a vital element of the soul's expression in life. To nurture, be grounded in and fully care for the body. To savor the physicality of the human experience. To explore how to fully embody the spirit in your body and to be committed and devoted to seeing how much life force you can embody into your physical form.

Gate	Traditional HD Gate Name	Quantum HD Gate Name	Shadow Aspect	High Expression
47	Realization	Mindset	To quit or give up an inspiration because you can't "figure out" how to make it happen. To feel defeated and broken because you think you have ideas that you can't manifest.	To engage in hopeful, inspired thoughts no matter what is going on around you. To use inspiration as a catalyst for calibrating emotional frequency and the Heart.
48	Depth	Wisdom	Paralysis in inadequacy. To be afraid to try something new or to go beyond your comfort zone because you think you don't know or that you're not ready.	The wisdom to explore and learn the depth of knowledge necessary to create a strong foundation for action and mastery. The self-trust to have faith in your ability to know how to know, and to trust your connection to Source as the true Source for your knowledge.
49	Principles	The Catalyst	Quitting too soon as a way of avoiding intimacy. Compromising on your value and upholding agreements that no longer serve you. Creating drama and fighting for outdated values that no longer serve the higher good.	The ability to sense when it's time to hold to a value that supports your value. The ability to inspire others to make expansive changes that embrace higher principles and a deeper alignment with peace and sustainability. The willingness to align with a higher value.
50	Values	Nurturing	To over-care. To let guilt stop you from sustaining yourself. To hold to rigid principles and to struggle to allow others the consequences of their choices.	The ability to nurture yourself so that you have more to give others. The intuition to know what others need to bring them into greater alignment with Love. To commit to higher principles that sustain in the name of peace and Love. To teach and share what you have to increase the wellbeing of others.
51	Shock	Initiation	To let the shock of disruption cause you to lose connection with your true purpose and with Source. To become bitter or angry with God. To try to control life and deplete yourself from the energy necessary to hold yourself back.	The ability to consciously use cycles of disruption and unexpected twists and turns of faith as catalysts that deepen your connection to Source and to your Life and Soul Purpose.

Gate	Traditional HD Gate Name	Quantum HD Gate Name	Shadow Aspect	High Expression
52	Stillness	Perspective	Attention deficit. To let overwhelm paralyze you and cause you to fail to act. To put your energy and attention in the wrong place and to spend your energy focused on something that bears no fruit.	The ability to see the bigger perspective and purpose of what is going on around you and to know exactly where to focus your energy and attention to facilitate the unfolding of what's next.
53	Starting Things	Starting	Reacting to the pressure to get an idea started. To feel like a failure because everything you start against right timing fails. To be afraid to start anything because of the trauma of your past "failures". Starting everything and never reaping the rewards of what you start.	The ability to sit with inspiration and be attuned to what the Inspiration wants and needs. To launch the initiation sequence for an idea and initiate it – and then let the idea follow its right course with trust in the flow.
54	Drive	Divine Inspiration	To react to the pressure that you have to fulfill an inspiration and to use force to push the inspiration into form – even though it might not be your idea/dream to manifest or the right time to bring it forth.	The ability to cultivate a deep relationship with the Divine Muse. To nurture the inspirational fruits of the muse, and to serve as a steward for an inspiration by aligning the idea energetically and preparing the way by laying foundational action and building.
55	Spirit	Faith	Indecisiveness. Fear and lack. Hoarding, keeping from others, fighting to take more than your share. Not trusting Source and drawing on Will to create.	The ability to hold the emotional frequency of energy and the vision for a creation. To trust in sufficiency so deeply that you're able to create without limitation.
56	The Storyteller	Expansion	To get lost or stuck in stories and narratives that are limiting. To tell stories that contract and deplete the energy of others.	The ability to share stories and inspirations that stimulate expansive and possibility-oriented thinking in others for the sake of stimulating powerful emotional energy that creates evolution and growth.
57	Intuition	Instinct	To be so afraid of the future that you are paralyzed. To not trust yourself and your own instinct. To know what needs to be done to prepare for the future and to fail to act on it.	The ability to sense when it is the right time to act. To intuitively know what needs to be made ready to be prepared for the future and to follow through on it.

Gate	Traditional HD Gate Name	Quantum HD Gate Name	Shadow Aspect	High Expression
58	Joy	Joy	To deny joy. To avoid the practice of mastery. To feel guilty or ashamed to do what you love. To disbelieve in joy.	To harness the joy of mastery and refine your practice until you reach fulfillment of your potential. To live in the flow of Joy.
59	Sexuality	Sustainability	To feel like you have to fight or struggle to survive. To feel the need to penetrate others and force your "rightness" on them. To let fear of lack cause you to craft relationships and agreements that are unsustainable.	To trust in sufficiency and to know that when you create abundance there is great fulfillment in sharing. To craft partnerships and relationships that sustain you and the foundation of your lives.
60	Acceptance	Conservation	To hold on and not allow for growth. To fight for the old and rebuke change. To let the overwhelm of change and disruption create paralysis and resistance.	The ability to find the blessings in transformation. Optimism. To know how to focus on what is working instead of what's not.
61	Mystery	Wonder	Allowing the pressure to know "why" to create bitterness or victimhood that is often perpetuated in a rationalized pattern.	The ability to see purpose in a bigger perspective that transcends the smaller details of an experience or event. Ability to stay in a state of innocence and confidence as a way of sustaining powerful creativity.
62	Details	Preparation	Fear and worry, Over-preparation. Allowing your plan to override the 'flow'.	The ability to be attuned to what is necessary to be prepared, and to trust that your alignment will inform you of everything that you need. Relaxing and knowing that you'll know what you need to know when you need to know it.

Gate	Traditional HD Gate Name	Quantum HD Gate Name	Shadow Aspect	High Expression
63	Doubt	Curiosity	Doubt (especially self-doubt) that leads to suspicion and the struggle for certainty. The unwillingness to question an old idea. The loss of curiosity.	The ability to use questioning and curiosity as a way of stimulating dreams of new possibilities and potentials. Thoughts that inspire the question of what needs to happen to make an idea a reality.
64	Confusion	Divine Transference	To feel pressure to try to "manifest" a big idea. To feel despairing or inadequate or ungrounded if you don't know how to make an idea a reality. To feel deep mental pressure to "figure" out an idea. To give up dreaming.	The ability to receive a "big idea" and to serve the idea by giving it your imagination and dreaming. To trust that you'll know how to implement the idea if it is yours to make manifest. To hold the energy of an idea for the world.

CONTEMPLATIONS

2024 REFLECTIONS

My wins from last year. How can I grow what I know is already working?

_____
_____
_____
_____
_____
_____
_____
_____
_____
_____
_____
_____
_____
_____
_____
_____
_____
_____
_____
_____
_____
_____
_____
_____
_____
_____
_____
_____
_____

2024 REFLECTIONS

JANUARY
2025

JANUARY

Monday	Tuesday	Wednesday	Thursday
		1	2
6	7	8	9
13	14	15	16
20	21	22	23
27	28	29	30

Friday	Saturday	Sunday	To-Do & Notes
3	4	5	**To-Do:** ○ ○ ○ ○ ○
10	11	12	○ ○ ○ ○ ○ ○
17	18	19	Notes
24	25	26	**JANUARY 2025**
31			**FEBRUARY 2025**

JANUARY 2025

Mo	Tu	We	Th	Fr	Sa	Su
		1	2	3	4	5
6	7	8	9	10	11	12
13	14	15	16	17	18	19
20	21	22	23	24	25	26
27	28	29	30	31		

FEBRUARY 2025

Mo	Tu	We	Th	Fr	Sa	Su
					1	2
3	4	5	6	7	8	9
10	11	12	13	14	15	16
17	18	19	20	21	22	23
24	25	26	27	28		

2025 INTENTIONS

Who will I be at the end of this year? Who do I need to be in order to fulfill my intentions for the year? How will I feel? What will my life look like? Write it out.

_____

_____

_____

_____

_____

_____

_____

_____

_____

_____

_____

_____

_____

_____

_____

_____

_____

_____

_____

_____

_____

_____

_____

_____

_____

_____

_____

_____

2025 INTENTIONS

What key actions do I need to take right now to begin the fulfillment of my intentions for this year my reality by the end of the year?

_____
_____
_____
_____
_____
_____
_____
_____
_____
_____
_____
_____
_____
_____
_____
_____
_____
_____
_____
_____
_____
_____
_____
_____
_____
_____
_____
_____

MONTHLY READING

Using divination cards of your choice, pull three cards to help you set your intentions for the month.
Get your own Quantum Cards at: **https://quantumhumandesign.com/quantum-cards**

CARD 1

What influences and lessons from the past need to be mastered to support my evolution?

_____

_____

_____

_____

_____

_____

CARD 2

What is my overarching theme this month that I need to pay attention to? What lessons does this card bring me?

_____

_____

_____

_____

_____

_____

CARD 3

What do I need to strengthen and master to move forward?

_____

_____

_____

_____

_____

_____

CONTEMPLATIONS

JANUARY 22, 2025

GATE 41: IMAGINATION

CHALLENGE:

To learn to use your imagination as a source of creative inspiration and manifestation. To experience the world and imagine more abundant possibilities. To stay connected to your creative fire.

AFFIRMATION:

I am a creative nexus of inspiration for the world. My ideas and imaginings inspire people to think beyond their limitations. My ideas stimulate new possibilities in the world. I am a powerful creator; my creative thoughts, ideas, and inspirations set the stage for miracles and possibilities that will change the story of humanity.

EFT SETUP:

Even though I am afraid my dreams won't come true, I deeply and completely love and accept myself.

EARTH:

Gate 31: Leadership

Explore this week what is your place of service? Who do you serve? What can you do to feel more empowered and influential in your life?

JOURNAL QUESTIONS:

◊ Do I own my creative power?

◊ How can I deepen my self-honoring of my creative power?

JANUARY 27, 2025

GATE 19: ATTUNEMENT

CHALLENGE:

To learn how to manage being a highly sensitive person and not let your sensitivity cause you to compromise what you want and who you are. To learn to keep your own resources in a sustainable state in order so that you have more to give. To not martyr yourself to the needs of others. To learn how to become emotionally intimate without being shut down or codependent.

AFFIRMATION:

I am deeply aware of the emotional needs and energy of others. My sensitivity and awareness give me insights that allow me to create intimacy and vulnerability in my relationships. I am aware and attuned to the emotional frequency around me and I make adjustments to help support a high frequency of emotional alignment. I honor my own emotional needs as the foundation of what I share with others.

EFT SETUP:

Even though it is scary to open my heart, I now choose to create space for deep intimacy and love in my life, and I deeply and completely love and accept myself.

JOURNAL QUESTIONS:

◊ Am I emotionally present in my relationships?

◊ Do I need to become more attuned to my own emotional needs and ask for more of what I want and need?

JANUARY 29, 2025

NEW MOON

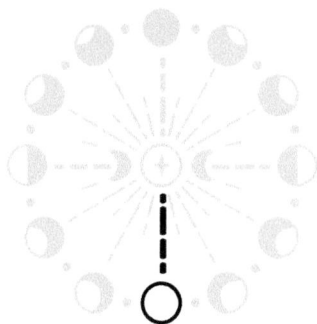

Aquarius 9 degrees, 50 minutes

Gate 19: The Gate of Attunement

New Moon energy invites us to explore how we can deepen our alignment with our intentions and asks us to focus on what we want to grow and expand on in our lives.

Welcome to the first New Moon of the Human Design year! The energies of the transits are electric with the pulse of new beginnings. You might find yourself eager and inspired to begin taking big steps toward what you want and need, but there's an interesting mix of energies in the celestial weather in combination with this New Moon.

The Gate 19 makes us deeply sensitive and dialed into our intuition and our awareness of what other people need. This can be a deeply emotional energy that makes us all feel like our emotions are on overdrive. It's important to guard yourself against being too empathic during this time, as it can often lead us to give up our own needs and wants for the sake of keeping others happy. Also, be mindful that when this energy transits, we'll all feel a little extra sensitive. Try not to take anything personally.

This New Moon offers a big invitation to explore the quality of your relationships and your relationship agreements - a big theme that will be coming up for all of us again and again this year. We are being called to rewrite our relationship agreements so they are more aligned with our values and our true wants and needs. It's time to stop trying to give up what you need and want and to boldly ask for your own fulfillment.

It's also an energy that represents our relationships with animals and the natural world. Getting out in nature or hanging out with your pets can help integrate and regulate intense emotional energy if it gets too much. The Moon is also inviting us to reassess our relationship with our own health and wellness, our diet, and what changes we may need to make in order to be in a better relationship with our bodies.

Take some time with this new moon to ground yourself with nature before you honestly assess the quality of your relationships. Set the intention to call in relationships that are truly honoring your value and your values. Take some time to imagine experiencing true emotional intimacy in your partnerships. Also, focus on creating a dynamic community of support for yourself and a healthy relationship with food, nature and the environment.

CONTEMPLATIONS:

◊ Are my relationships sustaining me? What needs to shift and change for me to create more support in my relationships? What more do I need to give? What more do I need to receive?

◊ What is my relationship with food and nourishment? Is my body needing a change in my diet? What does my body need?

◊ What practices do I have to ground myself in nature? How can I create a more sustainable relationship with the natural world? What needs to change?

_____

_____

_____

_____

_____

_____

_____

_____

_____

_____

_____

_____

_____

_____

_____

_____

_____

_____

_____

CHALLENGE:

To learn how to manage being a highly sensitive person and not let your sensitivity cause you to compromise what you want and who you are. To learn to keep your own resources in a sustainable state in order so you have more to give. To not martyr yourself to the needs of others. To learn how to become emotionally intimate without being shut down or codependent.

OPTIMAL EXPRESSION:

The ability to sense the emotional needs of others and your community and to know how to bring the emotional energy back into alignment with sufficiency and sustainability. The ability to be emotionally vulnerable and present to increase Heart to Heart connections.

JANUARY 29, 2025
NEW MOON

UNBALANCED EXPRESSION:

Being overly sensitive and shutting down or compromising your own needs and wants. Feeling disconnected from others as a way of coping with being overly sensitive. Being emotionally clingy or needy is a way of forcing your natural desire for intimacy.

AFFIRMATION:

I am an integral part of the cosmic plan. I live in harmony with my body. I use the resources that nature provides to sustain my physical health and wellness. Part of my health is building relationships and community that supports and nurtures me. I surround myself with people who truly see and value me and support my creative process. I am bold and honest about what I need and want, and the people in my life who truly love me support me in getting my needs fulfilled in a healthy and loving way.

MONTHLY REFLECTIONS

My wins from last month. How can I grow what I know is already working?

_____
_____
_____
_____
_____
_____
_____
_____
_____
_____
_____
_____
_____
_____
_____
_____
_____
_____
_____
_____
_____
_____
_____
_____
_____
_____
_____
_____
_____
_____

MONTHLY REFLECTIONS

FEBRUARY

FEBRUARY

Monday	Tuesday	Wednesday	Thursday
3	4	5	6
10	11	12	13
17	18	19	20
24	25	26	27

Friday	Saturday	Sunday	To-Do & Notes
	1	2	To-Do:
			○
			○
			○
			○
			○
7	8	9	○
			○
			○
			○
			○
			○
14	15	16	Notes
21	22	23	**FEBRUARY 2025**
28			**MARCH 2025**

FEBRUARY 2025

Mo	Tu	We	Th	Fr	Sa	Su
					1	2
3	4	5	6	7	8	9
10	11	12	13	14	15	16
17	18	19	20	21	22	23
24	25	26	27	28		

MARCH 2025

Mo	Tu	We	Th	Fr	Sa	Su
					1	2
3	4	5	6	7	8	9
10	11	12	13	14	15	16
17	18	19	20	21	22	23
24	25	26	27	28	29	30
31						

MONTHLY INTENTIONS

Who will I be at the end of this month? Who do I need to be in order to fulfill my intentions for the month? How will I feel? What will my life look like? Write it out.

_____
_____
_____
_____
_____
_____
_____
_____
_____
_____
_____
_____
_____
_____
_____
_____
_____
_____
_____
_____
_____
_____
_____
_____
_____
_____
_____
_____

MONTHLY INTENTIONS

What key actions do I need to take to make the fulfillment of my intentions for this month my reality by the end of the month?

_____

_____

_____

_____

_____

_____

_____

_____

_____

_____

_____

_____

_____

_____

_____

_____

_____

_____

_____

_____

_____

_____

_____

_____

_____

MONTHLY READING

Using divination cards of your choice, pull three cards to help you set your intentions for the month.
Get your own Quantum Cards at: **https://quantumhumandesign.com/quantum-cards**

CARD 1

What influences and lessons from the past need to be mastered to support my evolution?

_____

_____

_____

_____

_____

_____

CARD 2

What is my overarching theme this month that I need to pay attention to? What lessons does this card
bring me?

_____

_____

_____

_____

_____

_____

CARD 3

What do I need to strengthen and master to move forward?

_____

_____

_____

_____

_____

_____

CONTEMPLATIONS

FEBRUARY 2, 2025

CHALLENGE:

To forgive the past and redefine who you are each and every day. To tell a personal narrative that is empowering, self-loving, and reflects your value and your authentic self. To bear witness to the pain and narrative of others and offer them a better story that allows them to expand on their abundance and blessings.

AFFIRMATION:

The story I tell myself and the one I tell the world, sets the tone and direction for my life. I am the artist and creator of my story. I have the power to rewrite my story every day. The true story I tell from my Heart allows me to serve my Right Place in the Cosmic Plan.

EFT SETUP:

Even though I'm afraid to speak my truth, I now share the truth from my heart, and trust that I am safe, and I deeply and completely love and accept myself.

EARTH:

Gate 7: Collaboration

Make a list of all the times when your influence has positively directed and influenced leadership and important ideas. Stay open to working in teams or groups. Find support and encouragement in collaboration with others this week.

JOURNAL QUESTIONS:

◊ What stories about my life am I holding on to?

◊ Do these stories reflect who I really am and what I want to create in my life?

◊ What or who do I need to forgive in order to liberate myself to tell a new story?

◊ What secrets or stories am I holding for others? Do I need to release them?

◊ Write the true story of who I really am.

FEBRUARY 7, 2025

GATE 49: THE CATALYST

CHALLENGE:

To not quit prematurely, failing to start a necessary revolution in your life, to not hold on to unhealthy situations, relationships, or agreements that may compromise your value and worth.

AFFIRMATION:

I am a cosmic revolutionary. I am aligned with higher principles that support the evolution of humanity. I stand for peace, equity, and sustainability. I align with these principles, and I stand my ground. I do the work to create the intimacy necessary to share my values with others. I value myself and my work enough to only align with relationships that support my vital role.

EFT SETUP:

Even though my emotional response causes me to react/paralyze me, I deeply and completely love and accept myself.

EARTH:

Gate 4: Possibility

Take some time this week to contemplate new ideas and possibilities for your life. Dreaming and daydreaming support refining focus and alignment this week.

JOURNAL QUESTIONS:

◊ Am I holding on too long? Is there a circumstance and condition that I am allowing because I am afraid of the emotional energy associated with change?

◊ Do I have a habit of quitting too soon? Do I fail to do the work associated with creating genuine intimacy?

◊ What do I need to let go of right now to create room for me to align with higher principles?

FEBRUARY 12, 2025

FULL MOON

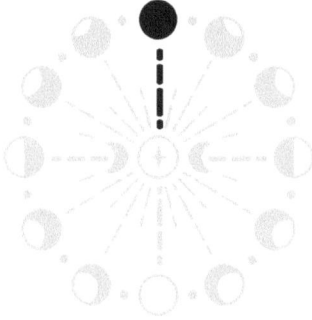

Leo 28 degrees, 43 minutes

Gate 4: The Gate of Possibility

Full moon energy invites us to explore what we need to release and let go of in order to stay in alignment with our intentions.

The energy with this Full Moon might feel a little intense. There's a lot of passion and opinions floating around in the cosmic weather, and it's easy to feel like people are shooting down your ideas. You may also feel a lot of pressure to manifest your ideas and can potentially feel like you've got to "figure out" how to make things happen quickly so that someone else doesn't take your idea.

Deep breath.

The purpose of the energy of this Full Moon is to explore what you need to release in order to embrace the possibilities you are imagining or dreaming about. This is NOT an energy that supports "figuring things out", but rather encourages us to take some time to dream and think about what else is possible. AND, while we're using the power of our imagination and dreaming to build fields

of information on a quantum level that will eventually manifest as new possibilities, we have to not let doubt - especially self-doubt - stop us from having big dreams.

Honor, nurture, and be a sacred steward of your dreams and ideas. Right now, they need you to take care of them. Spend time with them. Give them the gift of setting aside time to let them run wild through your brain with delusional confidence. This is the first key step to building the life you dream of. Don't worry if you don't have the answers about how you're going to make this happen right now. The details will handle themselves if you allow yourself to simply dream with this Full Moon. You don't have to figure it all out.

CONTEMPLATIONS:

◊ What keeps you from dreaming BIG? Do you have patterns of self-doubt that need to be released?

◊ What needs to be healed, released, aligned, and brought to your awareness to help you use the power of your dreams as your creative superpower?

◊ What are your big dreams?

◊ What needs to be healed, released, aligned, and brought to your awareness for you to trust yourself and believe in your dreams?

_____

_____

_____

_____

_____

_____

_____

CHALLENGE:

To learn to embrace ideas as possibilities, not answers, and to let the power of the possibility stimulate the imagination as a way of calibrating the emotions and the Heart. This Gate teaches us the power of learning to wait to see which possibility actually manifests in the physical world and to experiment with options in response.

This Gate also teaches us not to be doubtful if the idea doesn't manifest immediately or to turn doubt inward if we can't figure out how to make it a reality.

FEBRUARY 12, 2025

OPTIMAL EXPRESSION:

The ability to experience an idea as a possibility, to learn to use the idea as a "seed" for the imagination, and to use the imagination to create an emotional response which then calibrates the Heart and attracts experiences and opportunities that match the possibility into your life.

UNBALANCED EXPRESSION:

Self-doubt and fear that you have an idea you can't figure out. The pressure to try to share or implement the idea before it has had time to "seed" the manifestation. Acting too soon without waiting for the right timing.

_____

_____

_____

_____

_____

_____

_____

_____

_____

_____

_____

_____

_____

_____

_____

_____

_____

_____

_____

_____

_____

_____

_____

_____

_____

_____

_____

AFFIRMATION:

I am the sacred steward of my ideas and dreams. I don't have to figure out the "how" of my dreams. My job is to stay deeply rooted in my imagination and to use my power to envision my dream coming true as the vital first step in making my dream my reality. I nurture my ideas. I celebrate the possibilities and the potentials. I translate the pressure to figure out how to make my ideas a reality into an invitation to pause and simply allow myself to dream and imagine, knowing that my dreams are the due north on the compass of my life. The next right step will reveal itself with time, and I trust.

FEBRUARY 13, 2025

GATE 30: PASSION

CHALLENGE:

To be able to sustain a dream or a vision without burning out. To know which dream to be passionate about. To not let passion overwhelm you and to wait for the right timing to share your passion with the world.

AFFIRMATION:

I am a passionate creator. I use the intensity of my passion to increase my emotional energy and sustain the power of my dream and what I imagine for life. I trust in the Divine flow, and I wait for the right timing and the right circumstances to act on my dream.

EFT SETUP:

Even though my excitement feels like fear, I now choose to go forward with my passion on fire, fully trusting the infinite abundance of the Universe, and I deeply and completely love and accept myself.

EARTH:

Gate 29: Devotion

Who would you be and what would you choose if you gave yourself permission to say "no" more often? What would you like to say "no" to that you are saying "yes" to right now? What obligations do you need to take off your plate right now?

JOURNAL QUESTIONS:

◊ What am I passionate about? Have I lost my passion?

◊ How is my energy? Am I physically burned out? Am I burned out on my idea?

◊ What do I need to do to sustain my vision or dream about what I am inspired to create in my life?

◊ Do I have a dream or vision I am avoiding because I'm afraid it won't come true?

FEBRUARY 19, 2025

GATE 55: FAITH

CHALLENGE:

To learn to trust Source. To know that you are fully supported. To become proficient in the art of emotional alignment as your most creative power.

AFFIRMATION:

I am perfectly and divinely supported. I know that all my needs and desires are being fulfilled. My trust in my support allows me to create beyond the limitation of what others think is possible and my faith shows them the way. I use my emotional energy as the source of my creative power. My frequency of faith lifts others and opens up a greater world of potential and possibility.

EFT SETUP:

Even though I struggle with faith and trusting Source, I deeply and completely love and accept myself.

EARTH:

Gate 59: Sustainability

Notice your energy this week. Are you feeling vital and sustainable? If not, what can you do to rest and renew yourself this week?

JOURNAL QUESTIONS:

◊ Do I trust that I am fully supported? What do I need to do to deepen that trust?

◊ How can I align myself with abundant emotional energy? What practices or shifts do I need to make in my life to live and create in a more aligned way?

◊ Do I surround myself with beauty? How can I deepen my experience of beauty in my life?

◊ What do I have faith in now? What old gods of limitation do I need to stop worshiping?

◊ Go on a miracle hunt. Take stock of everything good that has happened in my life. How much "magic" have I been blessed with?

FEBRUARY 24, 2025

GATE 37: PEACE

CHALLENGE:

To find inner peace as the true source to outer peace. To not let chaos and outer circumstances knock you off your center and disrupt your peace.

AFFIRMATION:

I am an agent of peace. My being, aligned with peace, creates an energy of contagious peace around me. I practice holding a peaceful frequency of energy, and I respond to the world with an intention of creating sustainable peace.

EFT SETUP:

Even though I struggle to create peace and harmony in my life, I deeply and completely love and accept myself.

EARTH:

Gate 40: Restoration

We are grounded in rest, renewal, and reconnecting to our purpose this week. Take some time to truly nourish your body, mind, and spirit so that you have a full tank of energy reserves for the days ahead.

JOURNAL QUESTIONS:

◊ What habits, practices and routines do I have that cultivate my inner alignment with sustainable peace?

◊ When I feel that my outer world is chaotic and disrupted, how do I cultivate inner peace?

◊ What do I need to do to cultivate a peaceful emotional frequency?

FEBRUARY 28, 2025

Pisces 9 degrees, 40 minutes

Gate 37: The Gate of Peace

New Moon energy invites us to explore how we can deepen our alignment with our intentions and asks us to focus on what we want to grow and expand on in our lives.

This New Moon brings a lot of potential for chaos and disorder. You may find yourself feeling out of control and the temptation to try to control the uncontrollable may result in exhaustion and depletion. It's important with this New Moon to explore what you're actually in control of and what you may need to let go of in order to stay sustainable and to harness the energy you need to move forward.

The irony of the potential for chaos is that Gate 37 brings us the possibility of peace. But, peace is cultivated first on the inside. When we ARE peaceful then we create a vibrational field of peace, giving us the capacity to then create peace on the outside. In other words, hard as it may be right now, you must cultivate inner peace to create outer peace.

Embodying peace requires practice and since New Moon energy invites us to explore what needs to be started or initiated, this New Moon is inviting you to contemplate what practices you need to cultivate to strengthen your inner peace. Now is the time to strengthen your practice so that you become habituated and patterned - and you have the will - to stay grounded in your own peace no matter what is going on around you.

This New Moon is not only calling you forward to create your own inner experience of peace but inviting all of us to envision a world of peace. Take some time with this New Moon energy to imagine peace for our planet and for all sentient beings.

CONTEMPLATIONS:

◊ How peaceful do you feel?

◊ What do you need to do to strengthen your inner peace?

◊ What practices do you need to add to your life to strengthen your inner peace?

_____

_____

_____

_____

_____

_____

_____

_____

_____

_____

CHALLENGE:

To find inner peace as the true source of outer peace. To not let chaos and outer circumstances knock you off your center and disrupt your peace.

OPTIMAL EXPRESSION:

The ability to stay connected to sustainable peace and to respond to life by generating peace no matter what is happening in your reality. Creating the emotional alignment to make peaceful choices no matter what's going on in the outer world.

FEBRUARY 28, 2025

NEW MOON

UNBALANCED EXPRESSION:

Desperately struggling to find peace outside of yourself. Trying to control the outer world to create inner peace.

AFFIRMATION:

I choose peace. I strengthen and condition my inner environment to be peaceful so that I can respond intentionally and peacefully to the world around me. I hold a vision of a peaceful world and I act as an agent of peace with my every movement through this world. I cultivate a practice of being peaceful that allows me to anchor myself in peace, no matter what is going on around me. I am a source of peace for myself, for others, and for the world.

MONTHLY REFLECTIONS

My wins from last month. How can I grow what I know is already working?

_____
_____
_____
_____
_____
_____
_____
_____
_____
_____
_____
_____
_____
_____
_____
_____
_____
_____
_____
_____
_____
_____
_____
_____
_____
_____
_____

MONTHLY REFLECTIONS

MARCH

MARCH

Monday	Tuesday	Wednesday	Thursday
3	4	5	6
10	11	12	13
17	18	19	20
24	25	26	27
31			

Friday	Saturday	Sunday	To-Do & Notes
	1	2	To-Do:
			O
			O
			O
			O
			O
7	8	9	O
			O
			O
			O
			O
			O
14	15	16	Notes
21	22	23	**MARCH 2025**
28	29	30	**APRIL 2025**

MARCH 2025

Mo	Tu	We	Th	Fr	Sa	Su
					1	2
3	4	5	6	7	8	9
10	11	12	13	14	15	16
17	18	19	20	21	22	23
24	25	26	27	28	29	30
31						

APRIL 2025

Mo	Tu	We	Th	Fr	Sa	Su
	1	2	3	4	5	6
7	8	9	10	11	12	13
14	15	16	17	18	19	20
21	22	23	24	25	26	27
28	29	30				

MONTHLY INTENTIONS

Who will I be at the end of this month? Who do I need to be in order to fulfill my intentions for the month? How will I feel? What will my life look like? Write it out.

_____

_____

_____

_____

_____

_____

_____

_____

_____

_____

_____

_____

_____

_____

_____

_____

_____

_____

_____

_____

_____

_____

_____

_____

_____

_____

MONTHLY INTENTIONS

What key actions do I need to take to make the fulfillment of my intentions for this month my reality by the end of the month?

_____

_____

_____

_____

_____

_____

_____

_____

_____

_____

_____

_____

_____

_____

_____

_____

_____

_____

_____

_____

_____

_____

_____

_____

_____

MONTHLY READING

Using divination cards of your choice, pull three cards to help you set your intentions for the month.
Get your own Quantum Cards at: **https://quantumhumandesign.com/quantum-cards**

CARD 1

What influences and lessons from the past need to be mastered to support my evolution?

_____

_____

_____

_____

_____

_____

_____

CARD 2

What is my overarching theme this month that I need to pay attention to? What lessons does this card
bring me?

_____

_____

_____

_____

_____

_____

_____

CARD 3

What do I need to strengthen and master to move forward?

_____

_____

_____

_____

_____

_____

_____

CONTEMPLATIONS

MARCH 2, 2025

GATE 63: CURIOSITY

CHALLENGE:

To not let self-doubt and suspicion cause you to stop being curious.

AFFIRMATION:

My curiosity makes me a conduit of possibility thinking. I ask questions that stimulate imaginations. I allow the questions of my mind to seed dreams that stimulate my imagination and the imagination of others. I share my questions as an opening to the fulfillment of potential in the world.

EFT SETUP:

Even though I struggle with trusting myself, I now choose to relax and know that I know. I listen to my intuition. I abandon logic and let my Higher Knowing anchor my spirit in trust, and I deeply and completely love and accept myself.

EARTH:

Gate 64: Divine Transference

How can you embrace your dreams and stop judging them even if you don't know how to yet?

JOURNAL QUESTIONS:

◊ Am I curious about life?

◊ Do I regularly allow myself to be curious about what else is possible in the world? In my life?

◊ Do I doubt myself and my ideas?

◊ What needs to happen for me to unlock my need to be right about an idea and to allow myself to dream of possibilities again?

MARCH 7, 2025

GATE 22: SURRENDER

CHALLENGE:

To trust that your passions and deepest desires are supported by the Universal flow of abundance. To have the courage to follow your passion and know that you will be supported. To learn to regulate your emotional energy so that you have faith that everything will unfold perfectly.

AFFIRMATION:

I am a global change agent. I am inspired with passions that serve the purpose of transforming the world. I trust that my emotions and my passion will align me with faith and the flow of resources I need to do to fulfill my Life Purpose. When I let go and follow my passion, I am given everything I need to change the world.

EFT SETUP:

Even though it is hard to trust in my support, I now choose to trust anyway, and I deeply and completely love and accept myself.

EARTH:

Gate 47: Mindset

How can you cultivate more hope and optimism? This week practice enjoying all of your ideas for the sake of enjoying them without the expectation that you need to "figure out" how to turn those ideas into reality.

JOURNAL QUESTIONS:

◊ Where am I denying my passion in my life? Where have I settled for less than what I want because I'm afraid I can't get what I want?

◊ What do I need to do to fully activate my passion? What is one bold step towards my genius that I could take right now?

◊ Do I trust the Universe? What do I need to do to deepen my trust?

◊ Do I have a regular practice that supports me in sustaining a high frequency of emotional energy and alignment?

◊ What needs to be healed, released, aligned, and brought to my awareness for me to deepen my faith?

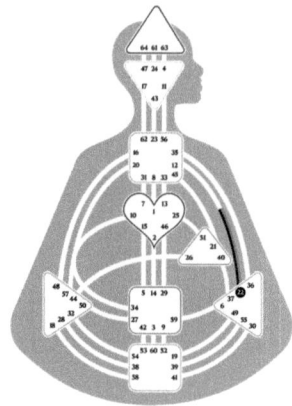

123

MARCH 13, 2025

GATE 36: EXPLORATION

CHALLENGE:

To not let boredom cause you to leap into chaos. To learn to stick with something long enough to become skillful and to bear the fruits of your experience.

AFFIRMATION:

My experiences and stories break old patterns and push the boundaries of the edge of what is possible for humanity. I defy the patterns and I create miracles through my emotional alignment with possibility. I hold my vision and maintain my emotional energy as I wait to bear the fruit of my intentions and my visions.

EFT SETUP:

Even though it is scary to be out of my comfort zone, I now choose to push myself into something new and more aligned with my Truth, and I deeply and completely love and accept myself.

EARTH:

Gate 6: Impact

Contemplate how you feel about abundance. List all the different ways you have been abundantly supported in the past.

JOURNAL QUESTIONS:

◊ How does boredom impact my life? What do I do when I feel bored? What can I do to keep myself aligned even when I'm bored?

◊ What stories have I experienced that have shattered old patterns and expectations? How have my stories changed or inspired others?

◊ What do I do to maintain or sustain emotional alignment? What do I need to add to my daily practice to amp up my emotional energy around my intentions?

MARCH 14, 2025
FULL MOON/TOTAL LUNAR ECLIPSE

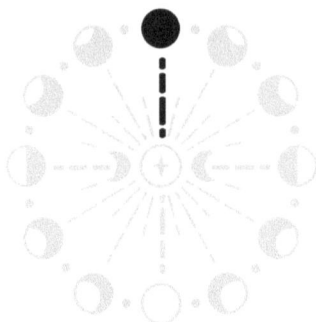

Virgo 23 degrees, 58 minutes

Gate 6: The Gate of Impact

Full moon energy invites us to explore what we need to release and let go of to stay in alignment with our intentions. Eclipse energy amplifies the intensity of the full moon, giving us an extra boost to let go and release!

We continue in this moon cycle with the theme of chaos and a need to cultivate inner peace in the face of disruption. Everything may be feeling a bit ratcheted up right now and it is up to us to impact others with our capacity to be deliberate and intentional versus reacting to circumstances that might be feeling emotionally charged.

This Full Moon invites us and the eclipse to explore what old ideas, beliefs, and even perceptions of scarcity we need to release in order to stay aligned with abundance and sustainability. We're also encouraged to look at how we need to better regulate ourselves so that we can serve as a resource for others during times that can feel intense and destabilizing. What habits, patterns, and mindset shifts do you need to make so that you can impact others in a more effective and sustainable way?

This is an emotional energy and an emotional time. Human Design teaches us that aligned emotional expression requires time. Take the time with this Full Moon to really feel your emotions and to process what you may be feeling to ensure that your response is truly intentional and deliberate and not reactive and potentially destructive.

The Gate 6 is one of the places in the Human Design chart where we hold the potential for fighting and war. But the opposite is also true. This is an energy that can support peace and sustenance. It is up to us to choose so we must choose wisely.

Take some time under the light of this moon to ask yourself what you want. Envision what you want and contemplate what you may need to release so that your approach to creating what you want is intentional, deliberate and abundant versus reactive and fearful. The more we align ourselves with the idea that we are enough and we have enough, the greater influence and impact we can have on our own lives and on the lives of others. Be a beacon of abundance.

CONTEMPLATIONS:

◊ What needs to be healed, released, aligned, and brought to your awareness to know that you are enough?

◊ What do you need to stay consistently emotionally regulated? What old ideas and beliefs do you need to release in order to stay emotionally aligned?

◊ What old beliefs about scarcity do you need to let go of?

CHALLENGE:

The ability to master emotional energy and learn to trust that your impact is in service to the world. When you understand that your life is a vehicle for service and your energy is being used to influence and impact those around you, you assume a greater obligation and responsibility to maintain a high frequency of energy. The quality of the emotional energy you cultivate influences others to come together in an equitable, sustainable, and peaceful way. Learning to trust that your words and impact will have an effect when the timing is correct and not overriding Divine Timing.

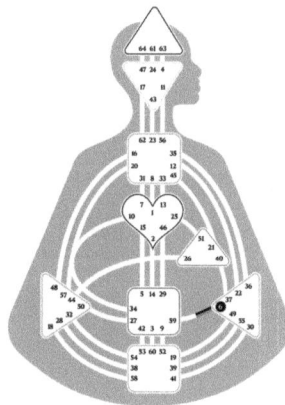

MARCH 14, 2025
FULL MOON/TOTAL LUNAR ECLIPSE

OPTIMAL EXPRESSION:

Maintaining a high frequency of emotional energy that supports equitability, sustainability, and peace. Using your emotional alignment to influence others and to serve as an energetic beacon of peace.

UNBALANCED EXPRESSION:

Feeling desperate, emotionally reactive, lacking, and invisible and being willing to do whatever it takes to take resources and energy for your own good, regardless of the means. Fear that you'll never be seen or heard.

AFFIRMATION:

I nurture and take care of my emotional well-being. I release old energy patterns out of my body so that I can respond with deliberation and intention to my own needs and to the needs of others. I am peaceful, and people turn to me for reassurance in times of upheaval. My emotional alignment and my sustainable energy are a resource to others, and my very presence influences the energy of the rooms I am in.

MERCURY
RETROGRADE CYCLE

March 15 – April 7

March 15 - Gate 21, the Gate of Self-Regulation
March 16 - Gate 17, the Gate of Anticipation
March 25 - Gate 25, the Gate of Spirit
April 2 - Gate 36, the Gate of Exploration

Retrograde cycles encourage us to go inward to explore the themes the planets give us. Mercury is the planet associated with communication. When Mercury goes retrograde it gives us an opportunity to go inward and contemplate how we can better align ourselves to have greater influence and impact in the world. Take your time to find the right words during this cycle. Do your best to not make big decisions, sign contracts, or make large purchases. Expect delays. Breathe and be patient with others (and yourself)!

The four Gates highlighted by this Mercury retrograde cycle are Gates that play out in the transits all year and highlight the importance of touching base with your higher purpose as a key element in helping you remember your value and your unique role on the planet.

We start with the energy for self-regulation, which, in the shadow, promises to reveal to us where we may be holding on and trying to control the uncontrollable. In the high expression, we're encouraged to examine our patterns and habits and so that we can be sure that we are constructing a daily practice that strengthens our resilience and allows us to serve our higher purpose.

As Mercury retrogrades through the Gate 17, we're exploring new options and thinking about better ways to structure our lives and habits. We're opening to new possibilities for ourselves and playing with new potentials for our lives.

When Mercury retrogrades through Gate 25, we're invited to get out of our heads, drop into our hearts, and ask Spirit the question, "What is mine to do in the world?" We're leaning in and exploring what needs to be aligned so that we are fulfilling our right place and taking up our right space in the world.

We finish this cycle before we enter the shadow, where we begin to integrate all the insights we've gleaned, journeying through Gate 36, where we're given an extra boost to break free from limiting patterns if we have faith in something bigger. We're on the edge of the new and releasing the old so we can begin a new cycle of expansion and alignment.

March 15

March 16

March 25

April 2

MERCURY
RETROGRADE CYCLE

CHALLENGE:

To trust the process. To allow yourself to know that you are a unique, vital, and irreplaceable part of the cosmic plan and that, literally, the world needs you to be who you were born to be so that you can play your important role. To know that this is not "ego" but just true for you and for all other humans on the planet. To trust that if you let go of old defensive patterns, you'll expand and grow and increase your capacity for more.

AFFIRMATION:

I am inherently valuable because I exist. I play a role on the planet that no one else can play. My very existence is essential to the evolution of the world. My worth demands that I untangle myself from patterns that keep me denying my value. I release old patterns that limit me and take quantum leaps of evolution.

OPTIMAL EXPRESSION:

To retreat and allow yourself to recalibrate your identity so that the story you tell yourself and the world about who you are and how you are is a match to what you want to be experiencing in life.

UNBALANCED EXPRESSION:

To try to control the uncontrollable or to feel controlled by others. To feel shamed and judged by others. To mistrust a higher purpose and feel stuck in victim consciousness. To allow emotions to drive your decisions and to create chaos as a result.

CONTEMPLATIONS:

◊ Who do I need to become to create what is yours to create?

◊ What needs to be healed, released, aligned and brought to my awareness for you to strengthen your connection with your purpose?

◊ Who do I need to be to transcend the patterns of history held in my identity that keep me playing small?

_____

_____

_____

_____

_____

_____

_____

March 15

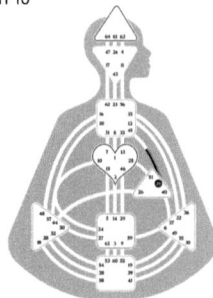

_____

_____

_____

_____

_____

_____

_____

March 16

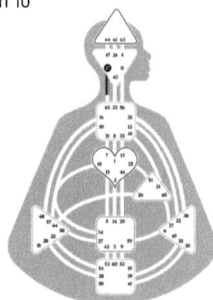

_____

_____

_____

_____

_____

_____

_____

March 25

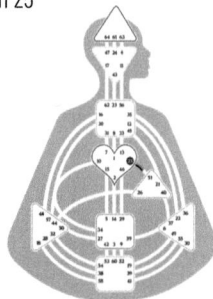

_____

_____

_____

_____

_____

_____

_____

April 2

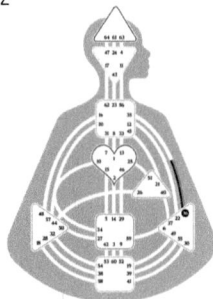

_____

_____

_____

_____

_____

_____

_____

MARCH 19, 2025

GATE 25: SPIRIT

CHALLENGE:

To trust the Divine Order in all of your life. To learn to connect with Source as the path to creating wellbeing in your life. To remember that your life serves an irreplaceable role in the Cosmic Plan and to honor that role and to live from it. To trust Source.

AFFIRMATION:

I am an agent of the Divine. My life is the fulfillment of Divine Order and the Cosmic Plan. When I am connected to Source, I serve my right place. I take up no more than my space and no less than my place in the world. I serve and through serving, I am supported.

EFT SETUP:

Even though in the past, I was afraid to follow my heart, I now choose to do what is right for me and know that I am fully supported, and I deeply and completely love and accept myself.

EARTH:

Gate 46: Embodiment

What do you need to do to better love and nurture your body? This week spend some time in front of the mirror and ask your body what it needs to embody greater vitality.

JOURNAL QUESTIONS:

◊   Do I trust Source?

◊   Do I have a regular practice that connects me to Source?

◊   Do I know my Life Purpose?

◊   Am I living true to my Purpose?

◊   How can I deepen my connection to my Purpose?

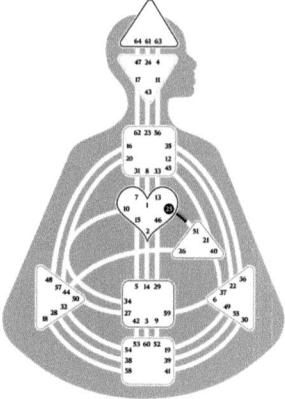

MARCH 24, 2025

GATE 17: ANTICIPATION

CHALLENGE:

To learn to share your thoughts about possibilities only when people ask for them. To not let doubt and suspicion keep you from seeing the potential of positive outcomes.

AFFIRMATION:

I use the power of my mind to explore possibilities and potential. I know that the inspirations and insights that I have create exploration and experimentation that can inspire the elegant solutions necessary to skillfully control the challenges facing humanity.

EFT SETUP:

Even though I have a lot of ideas and thoughts to share, I trust that the insights I have to offer are too important to blurt out and I wait for the right people to ask, and I deeply and completely love and accept myself.

EARTH:

Gate 18: Re-Alignment

This week explore where you need to add more joy to your life. Do you have any old stories you need to release around being "right?"

JOURNAL QUESTIONS:

◊ What do I need to do to manage my insights and ideas so that they increase the options and potential of others?

◊ How do I feel about holding back from sharing my insights until the timing is right?

◊ What can I do to manage my need to share without waiting for the right timing?

◊ What routines and strategies do I need to cultivate to keep my perspectives expanding and possibility-oriented?

◊ How can I improve my ability to manage doubt and fear?

MARCH 29, 2025

NEW MOON/PARTIAL SOLAR ECLIPSE

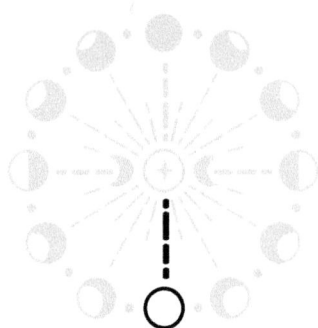

Aries 8 degrees, 53 minutes

Gate 21: The Gate of Self-Regulation

New Moon energy invites us to explore how we can deepen our alignment with our intentions and asks us to focus on what we want to grow and expand on in our lives. Eclipse energy amplifies the intensity of the New Moon.

Sometimes to really be able to regulate ourselves, we have to step back and look at the big picture to see what's really going on. When we're down in the weeds, it's easy to struggle with the daily actions necessary to fortify our resilience muscles. This New Moon invites you to do just that, take a step back, ground yourself in your higher purpose, trust the process, and keep taking the steps necessary to keep yourself aligned with the future you envision.

This is a powerful time to explore your arsenal of practices that you use for self-care and self-regulation. Take some time today to explore whether your inner and outer environment is self-generous and, if it's not, contemplate what changes you may need to make to ensure that you're creating an energetic and material matrix that supports you being able to stay the course and stay aligned with who you are and the bigger purpose of your existence.

Because this Gate and this New Moon theme is focused on Will Center themes, your ego is on the line. Be mindful of the need to try to prove your value or your desire to control others. You have nothing to prove. Your job on this New Moon/Solar Eclipse is to set the stage - with great intention - to live from your inner sense of value, to clarify your values, and to make sure that your daily practice of self-regulation is helping you live a life aligned with deeper meaning and purpose.

Remember, your life purpose is to fulfill the full potential of that unique, vital, and irreplaceable role only you can play in the cosmic plan. You are a once-in-a-lifetime-cosmic-event. What needs to happen for you to protect, proclaim, and defend your value and to live in total integrity with all of who you are? This is the BIG question to explore under this New Moon. How are you going to take care of all of who you are?

CONTEMPLATIONS:

◊ Where do you need to strengthen your capacity to self-regulate?

◊ Are you proud of who you are? Make a list of everything about yourself that you love and value.

◊ What new habits and patterns do you need to establish in order to strengthen your sense of your own value?

◊ Take some time under this moon and explore your higher purpose. Are you compromising on your purpose? What needs to shift in your life to deepen your connection to your life purpose? What new things need to be added to your life to strengthen your authentic self-expression?

_____

_____

_____

_____

_____

_____

_____

_____

_____

_____

_____

_____

_____

_____

_____

_____

_____

_____

_____

CHALLENGE:

To learn to let go. To master self-regulation. To release the need to control others and circumstances. To trust in the Divine and to know that you are supported. Knowing that you are worthy of support and you don't have to over-compensate.

OPTIMAL EXPRESSION:

The ability to regulate your inner and outer environment in order to sustain a vibrational frequency that reflects your true value. The ability to be self-generous and to set boundaries that maintain your value and support you in being sustainable in the world. To take the actions necessary to honor your unique role in the cosmic plan.

UNBALANCED EXPRESSION:

To feel the need to control life, others, resources, etc., out of fear that you aren't worthy of being supported.

MARCH 29, 2025
NEW MOON/PARTIAL SOLAR ECLIPSE

AFFIRMATION:

I am a unique, once-in-a-lifetime-cosmic-event. I am precious and valuable. I know my life is important and my well-being is essential to fulfilling my life purpose. I structure my life so that I sustain, nurture and regulate myself and my environment so that my daily habits and practices create structure for my fulfillment, sustainability and joy. I proclaim and defend my value by setting clear boundaries and creating a self-generous internal and external environment.

JOURNAL QUESTIONS:

◊ What do I need to do to manage my insights and ideas so that they increase the options and potential of others?

◊ How do I feel about holding back from sharing my insights until the timing is right?

◊ What can I do to manage my need to share without waiting for the right timing?

◊ What routines and strategies do I need to cultivate to keep my perspectives expanding and possibility-oriented?

◊ How can I improve my ability to manage doubt and fear?

MARCH 30, 2025

GATE 21: SELF-REGULATION

CHALLENGE:

To learn to let go. To become proficient at self-regulation. To release the need to control others and circumstances. To trust in the Divine and to know that you are supported. Knowing you are worthy of support and you don't have to overcompensate.

AFFIRMATION:

I am worthy of claiming, protecting, and defending my rightful place in the world. I create an inner and outer environment that is self-generous, and I regulate my environment to sustain a high frequency of alignment with my true value. I know that I am an irreplaceable and precious part of the Cosmic Plan and I create my life to reflect the importance of my right place in the world.

EFT SETUP:

Even though in the past I felt like I had to control everything, I now surrender to Source and know that my abundance, my TRUE abundance, is available to me when I let go and let the Universe do the work, and I deeply and completely love and accept myself.

JOURNAL QUESTIONS:

◊ Where do I need to release control in my life?

◊ Do I trust the Universe?

◊ Do I value myself? Do I trust that I will be supported in accordance with my value?

◊ What do I need to do to create an internal and external environment of self-generosity?

◊ What needs to be healed, released, aligned, and brought to my awareness for me to embrace my true value?

Gate 48: Wisdom

Make a list of all of your training, all of the skills you have and all of the knowledge you've gleaned from your life experiences. Take some time to truly acknowledge what you know.

MONTHLY REFLECTIONS

My wins from last month. How can I grow what I know is already working?

_____
_____
_____
_____
_____
_____
_____
_____
_____
_____
_____
_____
_____
_____
_____
_____
_____
_____
_____
_____
_____
_____
_____
_____
_____
_____
_____
_____
_____
_____

MONTHLY REFLECTIONS

APRIL

APRIL

Monday	Tuesday	Wednesday	Thursday
	1	2	3
7	8	9	10
14	15	16	17
21	22	23	24
28	29	30	

Friday	Saturday	Sunday	To-Do & Notes
4	5	6	**To-Do:**
11	12	13	
18	19	20	Notes
25	26	27	

To-Do:
- ◯
- ◯
- ◯
- ◯
- ◯
- ◯
- ◯
- ◯
- ◯
- ◯
- ◯

Notes

APRIL 2025

Mo	Tu	We	Th	Fr	Sa	Su
	1	2	3	4	5	6
7	8	9	10	11	12	13
14	15	16	17	18	19	20
21	22	23	24	25	26	27
28	29	30				

MAY 2025

Mo	Tu	We	Th	Fr	Sa	Su
			1	2	3	4
5	6	7	8	9	10	11
12	13	14	15	16	17	18
19	20	21	22	23	24	25
26	27	28	29	30	31	

MONTHLY INTENTIONS

Who will I be at the end of this month? Who do I need to be in order to fulfill my intentions for the month? How will I feel? What will my life look like? Write it out.

_____

_____

_____

_____

_____

_____

_____

_____

_____

_____

_____

_____

_____

_____

_____

_____

_____

_____

_____

_____

_____

_____

_____

_____

_____

_____

_____

_____

MONTHLY INTENTIONS

What key actions do I need to take to make the fulfillment of my intentions for this month my reality by the end of the month?

_____

_____

_____

_____

_____

_____

_____

_____

_____

_____

_____

_____

_____

_____

_____

_____

_____

_____

_____

_____

_____

_____

_____

_____

_____

_____

MONTHLY READING

Using divination cards of your choice, pull three cards to help you set your intentions for the month.
Get your own Quantum Cards at: **https://quantumhumandesign.com/quantum-cards**

CARD 1

What influences and lessons from the past need to be mastered to support my evolution?

_____

_____

_____

_____

_____

_____

CARD 2

What is my overarching theme this month that I need to pay attention to? What lessons does this card bring me?

_____

_____

_____

_____

_____

CARD 3

What do I need to strengthen and master to move forward?

_____

_____

_____

_____

_____

_____

CONTEMPLATIONS

APRIL 5, 2025
GATE 51: INITIATION

CHALLENGE:

To not let the unexpected cause you to lose your faith. Do not let a pattern of unexpected events cause you to lose your connection with your purpose and Source. To learn to use the power of your own story of initiation to initiate others into fulfilling their rightful place in the Cosmic Plan.

AFFIRMATION:

I navigate change and transformation with grace. I know that when my life takes a twist or a turn, it is my soul calling me out to serve at a higher level. I use disruption as a catalyst for my own growth and expansion. I am a teacher and an initiator. I use my ability to transform pain into growth and power to help others navigate through crisis and emerge on the other side of the crisis empowered and aligned.

EFT SETUP:

Even though things are not turning out like I expected, I now choose to embrace the unexpected and trust that the Universe is always serving my Greater Good, and I deeply and completely love and accept myself.

JOURNAL QUESTIONS:

◊ What has shock and the unexpected taught me in my life?

◊ How can I deepen my connection to Source?

◊ How can my experiences of initiation be shared with others? What am I here to wake people up to?

EARTH:

Gate 57: Instinct

Notice your intuition this week. What does your intuition feel like to you? Sometimes doing a retrospective analysis of your intuition/instinct makes it more clear how your intuitive signals work.

APRIL 10, 2025

GATE 42: CONCLUSION

CHALLENGE:

To learn to bring things to completion. To allow yourself to be led to where you need to be to finish things. To value your ability to know how to finish and to learn to give up your need to try to start everything. To finish things in order to create space for something new.

AFFIRMATION:

I am gifted at knowing when and how to finish things. I respond to bringing events, experiences, and relationships to a conclusion in order to create space for something new and more abundant. I can untangle the cosmic entanglements that keep people stuck in old patterns. My ability to re-align and complete things helps others create space for transformation and expansion.

EFT SETUP:

Even though I have hesitated in the past to finish what I needed to finish in order to make room for something new and better, I now choose to bring things to a powerful ending. I know that I am taking strong action to create space for what I truly want to create in my life, and I deeply and completely love myself.

JOURNAL QUESTIONS:

◊ Do I own and value my natural gift of knowing how to bring things to completion?

◊ What things in my life do I need to finish in order to make room for something new?

◊ Am I holding on to old circumstances and patterns because I'm afraid to let them go?

◊ Do I judge myself for not starting things? How can I learn to be gentler with myself?

EARTH:

Gate 32: Endurance

What actionable steps do you need to complete in order to be ready for creating what you want? Do one thing to lay the foundation for your dreams this week.

APRIL 13, 2025

FULL MOON

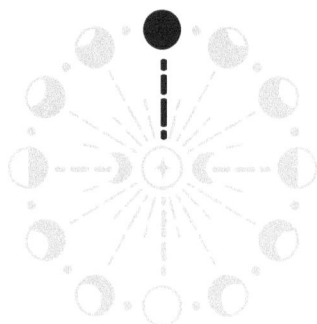

Libra 23 degrees, 19 minutes

Gate 32: The Gate of Endurance

Full moon energy invites us to explore what we need to release and let go of in order to stay in alignment with our intentions.

Right timing isn't an accident or some kind of magical thing that just happens. We can't always control time but we can influence and one of the most powerful things you can do to "speed things up" in your life is to be prepared for what you want.

What does that mean?

That means you must set the stage for creating what you want. For example, if you want to be a New York Times best-selling author, you can visualize and hope all you want, but if you don't actually write your book (or hire a ghostwriter), it's never going to happen.

Too often, we stop ourselves from being truly prepared to create what we want because we let our fear of failure stop us. We don't take the right actions because if we're not really prepared we can justify our failure. It's kind of like failing in advance.

This Full Moon invites you to release any fear of failure that might stop you short from actually doing what you dream of doing. How can you set the stage to receive and experience more?

CONTEMPLATIONS:

◊ What needs to be healed, released, aligned and brought to your awareness for you to allow yourself to be successful?

_____

_____

_____

_____

_____

_____

_____

_____

_____

_____

_____

_____

_____

_____

_____

_____

_____

_____

_____

_____

_____

_____

_____

_____

_____

_____

_____

_____

_____

_____

_____

_____

_____

_____

_____

_____

_____

_____

_____

_____

_____

_____

_____

_____

_____

_____

_____

_____

_____

_____

_____

_____

CHALLENGE:

To trust in Divine Timing. To prepare for the next step of manifestation and align with the unfolding of the process. To be patient.

OPTIMAL EXPRESSION:

The awareness of what needs to be done to make a dream a manifested reality. Setting the stage, preparation, being ready. The patience to trust that once the stage is set, the timing will unfold as needed to serve the highest good of all. To translate Divine Inspiration into readiness.

UNBALANCED EXPRESSION:

Letting the fear of failure cause you to avoid preparing what you need to do. To not be ready when the timing is right. To push too hard, too fast, and too long against right timing.

APRIL 13, 2025

FULL MOON

AFFIRMATION:

I have powerful, beautiful, and important things to do in life. These things are mine to do. I am a sacred steward of my dreams. I nurture my dreams by preparing the way for my dreams to be fulfilled. I am courageous and trust that if I am called to fulfill a dream, then it is mine to fulfill and the Universe provides me with divine support that ensures my perfect outcome. The more prepared and ready I am, the faster and easier it is to make my dreams come true.

APRIL 16, 2025

GATE 3: INNOVATION

CHALLENGE:

To learn to trust in Divine Timing and to know that your ideas and insights will be transmitted to the world when the world is ready.

AFFIRMATION:

I am here to bring change to the world. My natural ability to see what else is possible to create something new is my strength and my gift. I patiently cultivate my inspiration and use my understanding of what is needed to help evolve the world.

EFT SETUP:

Even though it is scary to take the first step, I now trust the Universe and my ability to be innovative and know that I stand on the cusp of the fulfillment of my Big Dreams. I deeply and completely love and accept myself.

EARTH:

Gate 50: Nurturing

This week practice taking care of yourself first—without guilt—so that you can better take care of others!

JOURNAL QUESTIONS:

◊ Where has Divine Timing worked out in my life? What has waiting taught me?

◊ Do I trust in Divine Timing?

◊ If the opportunity to share my ideas with the world presented itself today, would I be ready? If not, what do I need to prepare to be ready?

APRIL 22, 2025
GATE 27: ACCOUNTABILITY

CHALLENGE:

To care without over-caring. To allow others to assume responsibility for their own challenges and choices. To learn to accept other people's values. To not let guilt cause you to compromise what is good and right for you.

AFFIRMATION:

I have a nurturing and loving nature. It is my gift to be able to love and care for others. I know that the greatest expression of my love is to treat others as capable and powerful. I support when necessary, and I let go with love so my loved ones can discover their own strength and power.

EFT SETUP:

Even though it is hard to say no, I now choose to take the actions that are correct for me. I release my guilt, and I deeply and completely love and accept myself.

EARTH:

Gate 28: Adventure/Challenge

Where do you need to cultivate a sense of adventure in your life? Do one adventurous thing this week!

JOURNAL QUESTIONS:

◊ Am I taking responsibility for things that aren't mine to be responsible for? Whose problem is it? Can I return the responsibility for the problem back to its rightful owner?

◊ What role does guilt play in motivating me? Can I let go of the guilt? What different choices might I make if I didn't feel guilty?

◊ What obligations do I need to set down in order for me to take better care of myself?

◊ Are there places where I need to soften my judgments of other people's values?

166

APRIL 27, 2025

NEW MOON

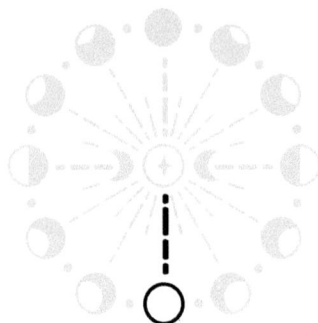

Taurus 7 degrees, 46 minutes

Gate 27: The Gate of Accountability

New Moon energy invites us to explore how we can deepen our alignment with our intentions and asks us to focus on what we want to grow and expand on in our lives.

We return again to a celestial theme that invites us to explore our relationships. Obligation and accountability are heavy energies but they're also beautiful energies. It is the heaviness of our obligations that can fulfill us. Think of parenthood or the fulfillment of nurturing your parents through the aging process. As difficult and exhausting as these tasks can feel in the moment, they are also part of what makes us human and defines our Hearts.

The energy of Gate 27 can be deep, rich, sacrificial when necessary and sustaining. The people we are obligated to are often the reason why so many of us do what we do. This energy anchors us in meaning and purpose. In the shadow it can also anchor us in depletion and guilt if we're not working with it correctly.

Sometimes, it can feel easier to do for others than to allow them to do for themselves. Sometimes, it's easier to pick up your child's toys for them than to empower them to do it themselves. This applies to all of our relationships. Interdependence strengthens growth and responsibility. Co-dependence weakens and is, ultimately, depleting.

This New Moon invites us to explore how we can begin again in our relationships so we assume responsibility for what is ours to provide. It also invites us to ask ourselves where we need to release responsibility for what does not belong to us. The most important question you can contemplate with this energy is, "Whose problem is it"? If it's not your problem, are you assuming responsibility for it and robbing someone of the gift of obligation and accountability?

The more you rebuild your relationships to be interdependent, the more sustainability and love you activate for yourself and those you love.

CONTEMPLATIONS:

◊ If you're struggling with an issue (or resentment) in a relationship, who does the problem in your relationship belong to? Are you assuming responsibility for something that isn't yours to be responsible for?

◊ What new responsibilities and relationship agreements do you need to make to create more energy or accountability for yourself?

◊ How can you release any guilt you may be holding that keeps you from letting go and setting healthy boundaries?

CHALLENGE:

To care without over-caring. To allow others to assume responsibility for their own challenges and choices. To learn to accept other people's values. To not let guilt cause you to compromise what is good and right for you.

OPTIMAL EXPRESSION:

The ability to support, nurture, and lift others up. To sense and act on what is necessary to increase the well-being of others and the world. To "feed" people with healthy food and healthy nourishment to ensure that they thrive. To hold others accountable for their own self-love and self-empowerment.

UNBALANCED EXPRESSION:

Codependency. Guilt. Over-caring. Martyrdom.

169

APRIL 27, 2025

AFFIRMATION:

I am a valuable partner in all of my relationships. I see the people I am in relationship with as capable, and I treat them that way. I make clear agreements and allow others to be responsible for their own choices and actions. The more I let go and allow, the more energy and unconditional love I receive.

APRIL 28, 2025

GATE 24: BLESSINGS

CHALLENGE:

To learn to allow what you truly deserve in your life. Do not rationalize an experience that allows for less than you deserve. To find the blessings and power from painful experiences and to use them as catalysts for transformation.

AFFIRMATION:

I embrace the Mystery of Life with the awareness that the infinite generosity of the Universe gives me blessings in every event in my life. I find the blessings from the pain. I grow and expand beyond the limitations of my experiences and stories. I use what I have learned to create a life and circumstances that reflect the miracle that I am.

EFT SETUP:

Even though it is scary to start something new... I am afraid I am not ready... I now choose to courageously embrace the new and trust that everything is in Divine Order, and I deeply and completely love and accept myself.

EARTH:

Gate 44: Truth

What patterns from the past are holding you back from allowing yourself to see and embody your true worth? What old patterns do you need to release this week?

JOURNAL QUESTIONS:

◊ What are the blessings I learned from my greatest painful experiences? Can I see how these experiences served to teach me? What did I learn?

◊ What am I grateful for from the past?

◊ Where might I be rationalizing staying stuck or settling for less than what I really want or deserve? What do I need to do to break out of this pattern?

MONTHLY REFLECTIONS

My wins from last month. How can I grow what I know is already working?

_____
_____
_____
_____
_____
_____
_____
_____
_____
_____
_____
_____
_____
_____
_____
_____
_____
_____
_____
_____
_____
_____
_____
_____
_____
_____
_____
_____
_____
_____

MONTHLY REFLECTIONS

MAY

MAY

Monday	Tuesday	Wednesday	Thursday
			1
5	6	7	8
12	13	14	15
19	20	21	22
26	27	28	29

Friday	Saturday	Sunday	To-Do & Notes
2	3	4	**To-Do:** ○ ○ ○ ○ ○
9	10	11	○ ○ ○ ○ ○ ○
16	17	18	Notes
23	24	25	**MAY 2025**
30	31		**JUNE 2025**

MAY 2025

Mo	Tu	We	Th	Fr	Sa	Su
			1	2	3	4
5	6	7	8	9	10	11
12	13	14	15	16	17	18
19	20	21	22	23	24	25
26	27	28	29	30	31	

JUNE 2025

Mo	Tu	We	Th	Fr	Sa	Su
						1
2	3	4	5	6	7	8
9	10	11	12	13	14	15
16	17	18	19	20	21	22
23	24	25	26	27	28	29
30						

MONTHLY INTENTIONS

Who will I be at the end of this month? Who do I need to be in order to fulfill my intentions for the month? How will I feel? What will my life look like? Write it out.

_____

MONTHLY INTENTIONS

What key actions do I need to take to make the fulfillment of my intentions for this month my reality by the end of the month?

_____

_____

_____

_____

_____

_____

_____

_____

_____

_____

_____

_____

_____

_____

_____

_____

_____

_____

_____

_____

_____

_____

_____

_____

_____

_____

_____

_____

MONTHLY READING

Using divination cards of your choice, pull three cards to help you set your intentions for the month.
Get your own Quantum Cards at: **https://quantumhumandesign.com/quantum-cards**

CARD 1

What influences and lessons from the past need to be mastered to support my evolution?

_____

_____

_____

_____

_____

_____

_____

CARD 2

What is my overarching theme this month that I need to pay attention to? What lessons does this card bring me?

_____

_____

_____

_____

_____

_____

CARD 3

What do I need to strengthen and master to move forward?

_____

_____

_____

_____

_____

_____

_____

CONTEMPLATIONS

MAY 3, 2025

GATE 2: ALLOWING

CHALLENGE:

To love yourself enough to open to the flow of support, love, and abundance. To incrementally increase over the course of your life what you're willing to allow yourself to receive. To learn to know that you are valuable and lovable simply because you exist.

AFFIRMATION:

I allow myself to receive the full flow of resources and abundance I need to fully express all of who I am. I recognize that my life is a vital, irreplaceable part of the cosmic tapestry and I receive all that I need because it helps me contribute all that I am.

EFT SETUP:

Even though I am scared because nothing looks like I thought it would, I now choose to relax, trust, and receive the support that I am designed to receive. I know that I will be supported in expressing my true self, and I deeply and completely love and accept myself.

EARTH:

Gate 1: Purpose

Spend time this week thinking about your Purpose and the gifts you long to give the world. How aligned are you with your Purpose?

JOURNAL QUESTIONS:

◊ Do I ask for help when I need it? Why or why not?

◊ Do I trust the Universe/God/Spirit/Source to support me in fulfilling my intentions?

◊ Am I grateful for what I have? Make a list of everything I'm grateful for.

◊ Can I transform my worry into trust?

◊ Do I believe that I deserve to be supported?

MAY 9, 2025

GATE 23: TRANSMISSION

CHALLENGE:

To recognize that change and transformation are inevitable. To know what needs to happen next, to wait for the right timing and the right people to share your insights with. Do not jump the gun and try to convince people to understand what you know. To not let yourself slip into negativity and despair when people aren't ready.

AFFIRMATION:

I change the world with what I know. My insights and awareness have the ability to transform the way people think and perceive the world. I know that my words are powerful and transformative. I trust that the people who are ready for the change I bring will ask me for what I know. I am a vessel for my knowingness, and I nurture myself while I wait to share what I know.

EFT SETUP:

Even though in the past I shut down my voice, I now speak my truth and offer the contribution of my unique spirit to the world, and I deeply and completely love and accept myself.

JOURNAL QUESTIONS:

◊ How can I strengthen my connection to Source?

◊ Do I trust what I know? What comes up for me when I know something, but I don't know how I know what I know?

◊ How do I handle myself when I know something but the people around me aren't ready to hear it yet?

EARTH:

Gate 43: Insight

This week, you're learning to trust your "knowingness." Practice trusting your inner knowing and the thoughts and ideas you have. Watch for self-doubt and don't discount what you "know" even if you don't know "how" you know what you know.

MAY 12, 2025

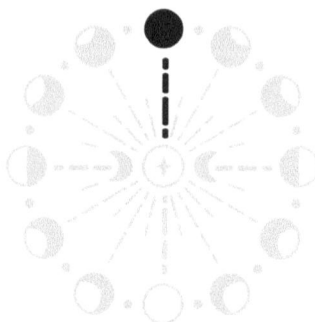

Scorpio 22 degrees, 12 minutes

Gate 43: The Gate of Insight

Full moon energy invites us to explore what we need to release and let go of in order to stay in alignment with our intentions.

The energy of this Full Moon can be tricky. We're getting inspired downloads. We can feel, sense, and know these downloads but they can feel elusive and difficult to explain to others. The inner knowing inspired by these downloads can sometimes leave us struggling to explain and often grappling with self-trust and confidence in what we know.

So much of this vital energy is related to time and timing. Trust your knowing but also trust that the time and timing to share what you know is a way to protect and nurture your own inner awareness and your power. What you know has the capacity to dramatically shift the way others think about things, but if you share what you know before they're ready - or before you're ready - you may either struggle to try to express what you know or you may find that other people react badly to your insights. Trust that when the time is right, the right person will ask you to share what you know, and it will transform both of you. There's a divine trajectory at play here.

The greatest challenge to this deep inner knowing is self-doubt. When we try to prove to ourselves HOW we know what we know or if we go down a deep rabbit hole of trying to justify what we know, we run the risk of discounting our own wisdom. This is a powerful Full Moon to explore where you may need to release any self-doubt keeping you from trusting your own inner knowing.

CONTEMPLATIONS:

◊ What needs to be healed, released, aligned and brought to your awareness for you to trust your inner knowing?

_____

_____

_____

_____

_____

_____

_____

_____

_____

_____

_____

_____

_____

_____

_____

_____

_____

_____

_____

_____

_____

_____

_____

_____

_____

_____

_____

CHALLENGE:

To be comfortable and to trust epiphanies and deep inner knowing without doubting what you know. To trust that when the timing is right you will know how to share what you know and serve your role as a transformative messenger who has insights that can change the way people think and what they know.

OPTIMAL EXPRESSION:

The ability to tap into new knowledge, understandings, and insights that expand people's understanding of the world. To align with the right timing and trust that you'll know how to share what you know when you need to share it.

MAY 12, 2025

FULL MOON

UNBALANCED EXPRESSION:

Feeling despair or frustration related to having knowledge but struggling to share what you know. Experiencing lighting bolts of knowingness and clarity but feeling overwhelmed by your inability to articulate what you understand. Not waiting for the right time to share what you know and feeling alone with your wisdom.

AFFIRMATION:

I know what I know, and I trust it. I treat my inner knowing with deep respect and nurture my thoughts and ideas as if they are sacred -which they are. I only share these precious insights with those who are ready and signify their readiness by asking me to share. When I am asked to share, if it feels correct and aligned, it allows me to transmit what I know. This sacred transmission solidifies my trust in myself and initiates the transformation necessary to reveal my next right step to me and to others.

MAY 15, 2025

GATE 8: FULFILLMENT

CHALLENGE:

To learn to express yourself authentically. To wait for the right people to see the value of who you are and to share yourself with them, with vulnerability and through all of your Heart. To learn to trust that you are a unique expression of the Divine with a purpose and a path. To find that path and to walk it without self-judgment or holding back.

AFFIRMATION:

I am devoted to the full expression of who I am. I defend and protect the story of my life. I know that when I express myself without hesitation or limitation, I AM the contribution that I am here to give the world. Being myself IS my Life Purpose, and my direction flows from my authentic alignment.

EFT SETUP:

Even though I question whether I have something of value to add to the world, I now choose to courageously follow the whispers of my soul and live a life that is a powerful expression of the truth of who I am. I speak my truth. I value my contribution. I know I am precious, and I deeply and completely love and accept myself.

JOURNAL QUESTIONS:

◊ Do I feel safe being vulnerable?

◊ What experiences have caused me to feel unsafe expressing my true self? Can I rewrite those stories?

◊ What would an uncompromising life look like for me?

◊ What do I need to remove from my current life to make my life more authentic?

◊ What is one bold action I can take right now that would allow me to express who I am more authentically in the world?

◊ What is my true passion? What do I dream of?

EARTH:

Gate 14: Creation

Ask yourself this week, "If I didn't need the money, what work would I be doing?" How is this work showing up in your life right now?

MAY 21, 2025

GATE 20: PATIENCE

CHALLENGE:

To be patient and control the ability to wait. To be prepared and watchful but resist the urge to act if the timing isn't right or if there are details that still need to be readied.

AFFIRMATION:

I am in the flow of perfect timing. I listen to my intuition. I prepare. I gather the experience, resources, and people I need to support my ideas and my principles. When I am ready, I wait patiently, knowing that right timing is the key to transforming the world. My alignment with right timing increases my influence and my power.

EFT SETUP:

Even though it is scary to not do anything and wait, I now choose to trust the infinite abundance of the Universe, and I deeply and completely love and accept myself.

EARTH:

Gate 34: Power

How can you cultivate greater patience while you're waiting? What fears come up for you when you think of waiting? How can you learn to wait with patience and ease and see "right timing" as power?

JOURNAL QUESTIONS:

◊ How do I manage my need for action? Am I patient?

◊ Do I trust in Divine Timing? Do I trust my intuition?

◊ What needs to be healed, released, aligned, and brought to my awareness for me to trust my intuition?

◊ What needs to be healed, released, aligned, and brought to my awareness for me to trust my intuition?

MAY 27, 2025

GATE 16: ZEST

CHALLENGE:

To learn to temper your enthusiasm by making sure you are prepared enough for whatever it is you are trying to do or create.

AFFIRMATION:

I am a faith-filled contagious force. I take guided actions and I trust my intuition and awareness to let me know when I am prepared and ready to leap into expanding my experience and genius. My enthusiasm inspires others to trust in themselves and to take their own giant leaps of growth.

EFT SETUP:

Even though I am afraid that I am not fulfilling my Life Purpose and I am wasting my life, I now choose to relax and know that I am in the perfect place at the perfect time to fulfill my destiny, and I deeply and completely love and accept myself.

EARTH:

Gate 9: Convergence

This week, explore your physical environment and ask yourself if there is something in it that is distracting you from your focus. What can you do to improve your environment? What can you do to increase your focus?

JOURNAL QUESTIONS:

◊ Do I trust my gut?

◊ Do I need to slow down and make sure I've done my homework before I take action?

◊ Have I sidelined my enthusiasm because other people have told me that I cannot do what I am dreaming of doing?

MAY 27, 2025

NEW MOON

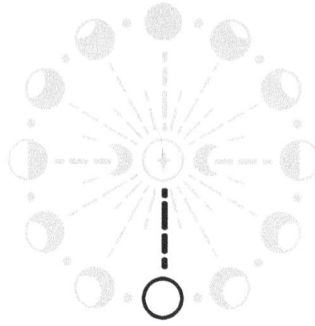

Gemini 6 degrees, 5 minutes

Gate 16: The Gate of Zest

New Moon energy invites us to explore how we can deepen our alignment with our intentions and asks us to focus on what we want to grow and expand on in our lives.

This New Moon gives us an extra shot of energy to start something new, but this same energy brings us a cautionary note. Like the Fool Card in the tarot deck reminds us, before you can start something new, you have to do your homework and be prepared. Without the right preparation, you run the risk of taking the first step on your new journey off the edge of a cliff. You need a map, a compass, a well-stocked rucksack, water, and a clear intention at the start of your journey. Without this, you may run full speed into chaos and disaster (and there's been plenty of that this year already!).

Zest is a juicy and inspiring energy. It's an energy that can get us unstuck when we've spent too much time down in the weeds tending to the infinite details. It sustains us when the going gets tough, but you have to work with it in a way that ensures its effectiveness. Zest without a path can be counterproductive. Zest with a plan can give you energy and endurance when the going gets rough.

This is New Moon energy, so it's a great time to start something - with ZEST - but be sure that you've laid the foundation for effective momentum before you leap without looking. (Also, use your zest responsibly. Make sure you're inspiring people towards an outcome rooted in well-being. Your zest can activate others. Make sure you're leading them towards something you're certain will work.)

Sometimes, especially during this transit, patience is necessary. Be sure to read the signs before you leap into action before it's time.

CONTEMPLATIONS:

◊ What are you excited about doing? Are you genuinely ready? If so, then now is the time to act.

◊ Have you done your "homework"? Do you need to make sure you've covered all the bases and are prepared for the next step? Is it the right time?

◊ Have you stifled your enthusiasm because it makes others uncomfortable? Where do you need to cultivate more zest in your life?

MAY 27, 2025

NEW MOON

CHALLENGE:

To learn to temper your enthusiasm by making sure you're prepared enough for whatever it is you're trying to do or create.

OPTIMAL EXPRESSION:

The courage to leap into action and to inspire others to act, even if you don't know all the details. The courage to trust your own intuition that the timing is right and you are "ready enough" even if you don't know exactly how your journey will unfold. Faith in the outcome.

UNBALANCED EXPRESSION:

Having a pattern of leaping into the unknown without sufficient preparation. Not assessing whether an idea or inspiration is actually an expression of Optimal Expression. "Leaping without looking." Holding yourself back when you know the time is right because others' tell you you're "not ready."

AFFIRMATION:

My zest, enthusiasm, and passion inspire others and give me the fuel to do amazing things. I use my zest with great intention, knowing that the spark of my essence is powerfully creative. I embrace my zest for life and express it fully when the time and timing are aligned. I am bold and don't hold myself back when it's the right time.

MONTHLY REFLECTIONS

My wins from last month. How can I grow what I know is already working?

_____
_____
_____
_____
_____
_____
_____
_____
_____
_____
_____
_____
_____
_____
_____
_____
_____
_____
_____
_____
_____
_____
_____
_____
_____
_____
_____

MONTHLY REFLECTIONS

JUNE

JUNE

Monday	Tuesday	Wednesday	Thursday
2	3	4	5
9	10	11	12
16	17	18	19
23 / 30	24	25	26

Friday	Saturday	Sunday	To-Do & Notes
		1	To-Do: ○ ○ ○ ○ ○
6	7	8	○ ○ ○ ○ ○ ○
1 3	1 4	1 5	Notes
2 0	2 1	2 2	**JUNE 2025** Mo Tu We Th Fr Sa Su 1 2 3 4 5 6 7 8 9 10 11 12 13 14 15 16 17 18 19 20 21 22 23 24 25 26 27 28 29 30
2 7	2 8	2 9	**JULY 2025** Mo Tu We Th Fr Sa Su 1 2 3 4 5 6 7 8 9 10 11 12 13 14 15 16 17 18 19 20 21 22 23 24 25 26 27 28 29 30 31

MONTHLY INTENTIONS

Who will I be at the end of this month? Who do I need to be in order to fulfill my intentions for the month? How will I feel? What will my life look like? Write it out.

_____

_____

_____

_____

_____

_____

_____

_____

_____

_____

_____

_____

_____

_____

_____

_____

_____

_____

_____

_____

_____

_____

_____

_____

_____

_____

_____

_____

_____

MONTHLY INTENTIONS

What key actions do I need to take to make the fulfillment of my intentions for this month my reality by the end of the month?

_____

_____

_____

_____

_____

_____

_____

_____

_____

_____

_____

_____

_____

_____

_____

_____

_____

_____

_____

_____

_____

_____

_____

_____

MONTHLY READING

Using divination cards of your choice, pull three cards to help you set your intentions for the month. *Get your own Quantum Cards at:* **https://quantumhumandesign.com/quantum-cards**

CARD 1

What influences and lessons from the past need to be mastered to support my evolution?

_____

_____

_____

_____

_____

_____

CARD 2

What is my overarching theme this month that I need to pay attention to? What lessons does this card bring me?

_____

_____

_____

_____

_____

CARD 3

What do I need to strengthen and master to move forward?

_____

_____

_____

_____

_____

_____

JUNE 2, 2025

GATE 35: EXPERIENCE

CHALLENGE:

To not let experience lead to feeling jaded or bored. To have the courage to share what you know from your experience. To know which experiences are worth participating in. To let your natural ability to become accomplished at anything keep you from being enthusiastic about learning something new. To embrace that even though you know how to know, you don't know everything.

AFFIRMATION:

I am an experienced, wise, and knowledgeable resource for others. My experiences in life have added to the rich tapestry that is the story of humanity. I share my stories with others because my experiences open doorways of possibility for others. My stories help others create miracles in their lives.

EFT SETUP:

Even though in the past I struggled to stay focused and move forward, I now trust myself to take the next steps on manifesting my dream. I am focused, clear, and moving forward, and I deeply and completely love and accept myself.

JOURNAL QUESTIONS:

◊ Where am I finding passion in my life? Do I need to create or discover more passion in my life right now?

◊ Do I share my knowledge and the stories of my experiences? Do I see the value of what I have to share?

◊ What am I curious about? How can I expand on that curiosity?

EARTH:

Gate 5: Consistency

Do something symbolic this week that represents order and establishing order in your life. Clean a closet, sort through your purse or wallet. A good week to take stock of your habits and explore what habits might need a little refreshing or tweaking.

JUNE 8, 2025
GATE 45: DISTRIBUTION

CHALLENGE:

To share and use your resources for the greater good of the whole. To learn to manage resources judiciously so that they benefit the greatest number of people. To teach as a pathway of sharing.

AFFIRMATION:

I am a teacher and a leader. I use my resources, my knowledge, and my experience to expand the resources, knowledge, and experiences of others. I use my blessings of abundance to increase the blessings of others. I know that I am a vehicle of wisdom and knowledge. I sense when it is right for me to share who I am and what I know with others.

EFT SETUP:

Even though I'm afraid to look at my finances, I now choose to take a real look at my financial numbers and know that awareness is the first step to increasing my financial status, and I deeply and completely love and accept myself.

EARTH:

Gate 26: Integrity

Where might you be experiencing a breach in your moral, identity, physical, resource, or energetic integrity? What do you need to do to bring yourself back into integrity?

JOURNAL QUESTIONS:

◊   Do I like to share? What do I have to give the world?

◊   How do I own my right leadership? Am I comfortable as a leader?

◊   Do I shrink from leadership? Do I overcompensate by pushing too hard with my leadership?

◊   Do I trust that when the right people are ready, I will be pressed into action as a leader and a teacher?

◊   What do I need to heal, release, align or bring to my awareness to trust my leadership energy more?

JUNE 11, 2025

FULL MOON

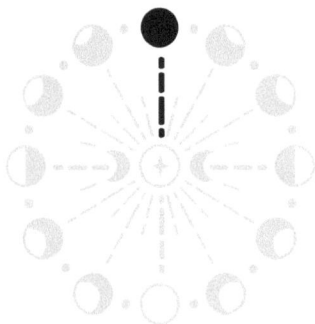

Sagittarius 20 degrees, 38 minutes
Gate 26: The Gate of Integrity

Full moon energy invites us to explore what we need to release and let go of in order to stay in alignment with our intentions.

This Full Moon invites us to start with the assumption that the Universe delivers to you exactly what you desire, provided that what you seek is in alignment with your self-worth and your authentic self. If you're trying to create something in an attempt to prove your worth because you doubt your value, you may experience many blocks and frustrations that can ultimately lead to burnout and other challenges.

Gate 26 is a place in our energy map associated with important aspects of the immune system. If we have in any way internalized the message that it's not okay or safe for us to be who we are and how we are, it can impact our immune system and our integrity. This is also the place in the chart where we can store trauma, and if the trauma is not resolved, we can get stuck in repeated patterns of self-defense that leave us playing small and struggling.

Human Design shows us that our sense of self-worth is rooted in integrity. There are five kinds of integrity in the Human Design chart. If we question our value, we may also experience a breach in any of these five areas of integrity.

The five kinds of integrity are:

1. Physical Integrity is experienced when our bodies are healthy and vital.

2. Resource Integrity is when we use our material resources in sustainable ways.

3. Identity Integrity is experienced when we feel that we can fully manifest the value of our authentic identity and we don't compromise who we are for the sake of money.

4. Moral Integrity is the courage to do the right thing and to make sure that our actions are honest and aligned with high principles and values.

5. Energetic Integrity is experienced when we consistently and deliberately rest and take care of ourselves so we have the energy to engage with life in a sustainable way.

If we doubt our value, we can experience disruption in any or even all of these key areas of integrity. This Full Moon invites you to explore what you need to release to heal your self-worth and what patterns need to be disrupted in order for you to bring yourself into greater harmony with the preciousness of who you were born to be.

CONTEMPLATIONS:

What needs to be healed, released, aligned, and brought to your awareness so that you truly know your value?

_____

_____

_____

_____

_____

_____

_____

_____

_____

_____

_____

_____

_____

_____

_____

_____

_____

_____

_____

_____

_____

_____

_____

CHALLENGE:

To learn to value your right place and your value enough to act as if you are precious. To heal past traumas and elevate your self-worth. To trust in support enough to do the right thing and to nurture yourself so you have more to give.

OPTIMAL EXPRESSION:

To live in moral, energetic, identity, physical, and resource integrity with courage and trust. To set clear boundaries and take the actions necessary to preserve the integrity of your right place.

UNBALANCED EXPRESSION:

To compromise your integrity because you feel or are afraid that you can't afford to fulfill your right place.

JUNE 11, 2025

FULL MOON

AFFIRMATION:

I am a unique, vital, and irreplaceable part of the cosmic plan. I am inherently valuable simply because I exist. My existence is precious and deserves to be protected. I act with integrity because I know I deserve to fully embody all of who I am. I am safe. I am enough. I have enough. The world needs me to be who I was born to be.

JUNE 13, 2025

GATE 12: THE CHANNEL

CHALLENGE:

To honor the self enough to wait for the right time and mood to speak. To know that shyness is actually a signal that the timing is not right to share transformational insights and expressions. When the timing IS right, to have the courage to share what you feel and sense. To honor the fact that your voice and the words you offer are a direct connection to Source and you channel the potential for transformation. To own your creative power.

AFFIRMATION:

I am a creative being. My words, my self-expression, my creative offerings have the power to change the way people see and understand the world. I am a vessel of Divine Transformation and I serve Source through the words that I share. I wait for the right timing, and when I am aligned with timing and flow, my creativity creates beauty and grace in the world. I am a Divine Channel, and I trust that the words that I serve will open the Hearts of others.

JOURNAL QUESTIONS:

◊ How has shyness caused me to judge myself?

◊ What do I need to do to cultivate a deeper connection with Source?

◊ What do I need to do to connect more deeply with my creative power?

EFT SETUP:

Even though I am afraid that I am failing my Life Purpose and mission, I now choose to know that I am in the right place fulfilling my right purpose. All I need to do is to follow my strategy, be deliberate, follow my heart, and all will be exactly as it needs to be, and I deeply and completely love and accept myself.

EARTH:

Gate 11: The Conceptualist

Get a blank notebook and train yourself to get into the habit of writing down all of your ideas. Nurture these ideas. Dream about them. Fantasize about them and see what shows up in your life in response.

JUNE 19, 2025

GATE 15: COMPASSION

CHALLENGE:

To learn to allow yourself to be in the flow of your own rhythm. Do not beat yourself up because you don't have daily habits. To have the courage to do the right thing even if you are worried about not having enough. To share from the Heart without giving up your Heart and serving as a martyr.

AFFIRMATION:

Like the power of a hurricane to transform the shoreline, my unique rhythm brings change to the landscape of my life and the world around me. I embrace my own rhythm and acknowledge the power of my own Heart. I share with ease, and I serve my own Heart as the foundation of all I have to give the world.

EFT SETUP:

Even though I feel powerless to make a difference in the world, I now choose to follow my heart and my passion knowing that I am the greatest gift I can give the world. The more I show up as my true self, the more I empower others to do the same, and I deeply and completely love and accept myself.

EARTH:

Gate 10: Self-Love

This week focus on nurturing yourself. What can you do to express love and appreciation for yourself?

JOURNAL QUESTIONS:

◊ Do I trust my own rhythm?

◊ Do I share from the Heart?

◊ Do I over share?

◊ Does my sharing compromise my own Heart?

◊ Do I judge my own rhythm?

◊ Can I find peace in aligning with my own rhythm?

◊ What old patterns do I need to break?

JUNE 25, 2025

GATE 52: PERSPECTIVE

CHALLENGE:

To learn to stay focused even when you're overwhelmed by a bigger perspective. To see the big picture, to not let the massive nature of what you know confuse you and cause you to struggle with where to put your energy and attention.

AFFIRMATION:

I am like the eagle soaring above the land. I see the entirety of what needs to happen to facilitate the evolution of the world. I use my perspective to see my unique and irreplaceable role in the Cosmic Plan. I see relationships and patterns that others do not always see. My perspective helps us all to build a peaceful world more effectively and in a consciously directed way.

EFT SETUP:

Even though it makes me nervous to stop "doing" and sit with the stillness, I now trust the process and know that my state of alignment and clarity with my intentions is the most powerful thing I can do to create effectively and powerfully in my life. I relax, I trust and let my abundance unfold, and I deeply and completely love and accept myself.

JOURNAL QUESTIONS:

◊ What do I do to maintain and sustain my focus?

◊ Is there anything in my environment or my life that I need to move out of the way in order for me to deepen my focus?

◊ How do I manage feeling overwhelmed?

◊ What things am I avoiding because I feel overwhelmed by them?

◊ What is one bold action I can take to begin clearing the path for action?

◊ How does my feeling of being overwhelmed affect my self-worth?

◊ How can I love myself more deeply in spite of feeling overwhelmed?

Gate 58: Joy

Do at least five things this week simply for the joy of it. Notice how joy feels and commit to cultivating more joy in your daily practice.

JUNE 25, 2025

NEW MOON

Cancer 4 degrees, 7 minutes

Gate 52: The Gate of Perspective

New Moon energy invites us to explore how we can deepen our alignment with our intentions and asks us to focus on what we want to grow and expand on in our lives.

This New Moon promises to bring a bit of sweetness and respite into your life if you use this energy correctly. Sometimes we just have to sit and rest. It is from this stillness we can often access the bigger viewpoint that allows us to refocus our efforts and enhance our creative power. Taking a step back is often what's necessary to create more forward momentum. This is a time to pause, rest, and enter into the void with great curiosity and an intention to see beyond the stress and pressure of the immediate moment and simply allow the process to unfold.

It's important not to resist this pause. If you don't take advantage of the clarity this moon is bringing you, you might find yourself overwhelmed and approaching life in frenetic spaghetti-throwing mode, leaving you exhausted and frustrated.

Do it. Take the pause. The payoff will be great.

CONTEMPLATIONS:

◊ Where do you need to create pauses in your life on a consistent basis?

◊ What is the bigger "why" behind what you're doing?

◊ How can you connect more consistently with your bigger purpose?

◊ If you could break down everything you need to do into smaller, more manageable steps, what would be one simple, small step you could take today?

_____
_____
_____
_____
_____
_____
_____
_____
_____
_____
_____
_____
_____
_____
_____
_____
_____
_____
_____
_____
_____
_____
_____
_____
_____
_____
_____
_____
_____
_____
_____
_____

CHALLENGE:

To learn to stay focused even when you're overwhelmed by a bigger perspective. To see the "big picture" and not let the massive nature of what you know confuse you and cause you to struggle with where to put your energy and attention.

OPTIMAL EXPRESSION: The ability to see the bigger perspective and purpose of what is going on around you and to know exactly where to focus your energy and attention to facilitate the unfolding of what's next.

UNBALANCED EXPRESSION:

Attention deficit. To let "overwhelm" paralyze you and cause you to fail to act. To put your energy and attention in the wrong place and to spend your energy focused on something that bears no fruit.

JUNE 25, 2025
NEW MOON

AFFIRMATION:

I am like an eagle soaring over a field. This perspective allows me to see the big picture of all that I am and all that I do. When I take a step back, pause, rest, and refocus my perspective, it is easier to see the essential actions I need to take. I relax and trust that each step leads to the next step, the next step, and the next. The process is unfolding exactly as it needs to, even if I can't see all of it at this time.

MONTHLY REFLECTIONS

My wins from last month. How can I grow what I know is already working?

_____

_____

_____

_____

_____

_____

_____

_____

_____

_____

_____

_____

_____

_____

_____

_____

_____

_____

_____

_____

_____

_____

_____

_____

_____

_____

_____

_____

_____

_____

MONTHLY REFLECTIONS

JULY

JULY

Monday	Tuesday	Wednesday	Thursday
	1	2	3
7	8	9	10
14	15	16	17
21	22	23	24
28	29	30	31

Friday	Saturday	Sunday	To-Do & Notes
4	5	6	To-Do: ○ ○ ○ ○ ○
11	12	13	○ ○ ○ ○ ○ ○
18	19	20	Notes
25	26	27	

JULY 2025

Mo	Tu	We	Th	Fr	Sa	Su
	1	2	3	4	5	6
7	8	9	10	11	12	13
14	15	16	17	18	19	20
21	22	23	24	25	26	27
28	29	30	31			

AUGUST 2025

Mo	Tu	We	Th	Fr	Sa	Su
				1	2	3
4	5	6	7	8	9	10
11	12	13	14	15	16	17
18	19	20	21	22	23	24
25	26	27	28	29	30	31

MONTHLY INTENTIONS

Who will I be at the end of this month? Who do I need to be in order to fulfill my intentions for the month? How will I feel? What will my life look like? Write it out.

_____

_____

_____

_____

_____

_____

_____

_____

_____

_____

_____

_____

_____

_____

_____

_____

_____

_____

_____

_____

_____

_____

_____

_____

_____

_____

_____

_____

_____

MONTHLY INTENTIONS

What key actions do I need to take to make the fulfillment of my intentions for this month my reality by the end of the month?

_____

_____

_____

_____

_____

_____

_____

_____

_____

_____

_____

_____

_____

_____

_____

_____

_____

_____

_____

_____

_____

_____

_____

_____

_____

_____

_____

_____

MONTHLY READING

Using divination cards of your choice, pull three cards to help you set your intentions for the month.
Get your own Quantum Cards at: **https://quantumhumandesign.com/quantum-cards**

CARD 1

What influences and lessons from the past need to be mastered to support my evolution?

_____

_____

_____

_____

_____

_____

CARD 2

What is my overarching theme this month that I need to pay attention to? What lessons does this card
bring me?

_____

_____

_____

_____

_____

_____

CARD 3

What do I need to strengthen and master to move forward?

_____

_____

_____

_____

_____

_____

CONTEMPLATIONS

JULY 1, 2025
GATE 39: RECALIBRATION

CHALLENGE:

To challenge and tease out energies that are not in alignment with faith and abundance. To bring them to awareness and to use them as pushing off points to deepen faith and trust in Source.

AFFIRMATION:

I am deeply calibrated with my faith. I trust that I am fully supported. I use experiences that create desire and wanting in me as opportunities to deepen my faith that I will receive and create all that I need to fulfill my mind, body, and spirit. I am in the perfect flow of abundance, and I am deeply aligned with Source.

EFT SETUP:

Even though I worry about money, having the right relationship, and creating abundance in every area of my life, I now trust Spirit and allow the abundant nature of the Universe to reveal itself to me. I stay open to the possibilities of miracles and trust that all I have to do is stay conscious of the abundance of Spirit unfolding within me, and I deeply and completely love and accept myself.

JOURNAL QUESTIONS:

◊ Do I trust Source?

◊ What do I need to do to deepen my trust in Source?

◊ Do I feel like I am enough?

◊ Do I feel like I have enough?

◊ Take stock of everything I have and everything I've been given. Do I have enough? Have I ever not been supported?

◊ What do I have that I'm grateful for?

◊ Have I abdicated my own power to create?

◊ What needs to be healed, released, aligned, or brought to my awareness to reactivate my power to create my own abundance?

EARTH:

Gate 38: The Visionary

One of the biggest things that can shut you down and cause you to procrastinate is not having a big enough dream. If you were going to blow the edges and limitations off of your dream, what would you create with your life? What is your really, really big dream? Spend some time imagining the fulfillment of your dream this week.

JULY 7, 2025

GATE 53: STARTING

CHALLENGE:

To respond in alignment with your energy blueprint to opportunities to get things started. To initiate the process of preparing or "setting the state" for the manifestation of a dream before it becomes a reality. To learn to trust in the timing of the Universe and not take charge and try to implement your own ideas while working against Divine Timing. To not burn out trying to complete things. To find peace as a "starter," not a "finisher."

AFFIRMATION:

I am a servant to Divine Inspiration. My thoughts, inspirations, and ideas set the stage for creative expansion and the potential for evolution. I take action on the ideas that present themselves to me in an aligned way. I honor all other ideas knowing that my gift is in the spark of energy that gets things rolling when the timing is right. While I wait for right timing, I guard my energy and charge my battery so that I am sustainable when the time is right for action.

EFT SETUP:

Even though I am scared to believe that my big dreams could come true, I now choose to trust the infinite power of the Universe and know that I am never given a dream that can't be fulfilled, and I deeply and completely love and accept myself.

JOURNAL QUESTIONS:

◊ How do I feel about myself when I have an idea and I can't get it initiated?

◊ How do I feel when someone takes my initial idea and builds on it?

◊ Do I value what I started?

◊ What identities and attachments do I have to being the one who starts and finishes something?

◊ Do I judge myself for not finishing something?

◊ How can I be gentler with myself?

◊ Do I trust Divine Timing?

◊ How can I deepen my trust in right timing?

EARTH:

Gate 54: Divine Inspiration

Is there anything you need to do or prepare to be ready for the next step in manifesting your dream, or inspiration?

249

JULY 10, 2025

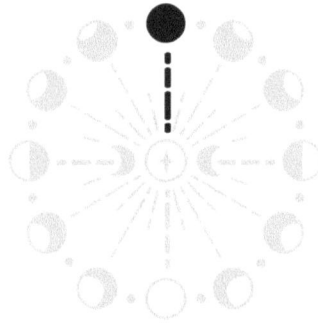

Capricorn 18 degrees, 49 minutes

Gate 54: The Gate of Divine Inspiration

Full moon energy invites us to explore what we need to release and let go of in order to stay in alignment with our intentions.

Inspiration married with action leads to right timing. Inspiration without aligned action leads to stagnation and stuck energy. This full moon issues an invitation to again review your relationship with time and timing. IF you feel frustrated because it seems things aren't happening fast enough, it might be time to take a short stroll to the bathroom mirror and have a heart-to-heart conversation with yourself.

When we act from our minds and force things into being based on what we think we "should" be doing or on what we learned somewhere, and those ideas lack that soul-deep, bone-deep knowing that comes from divine connection, these ideas rarely, if ever, bear fruit.

To cultivate right timing, your inspiration has to be sourced from a consistent and patterned connection with your Muse. In other words, you need to be sitting, journaling, meditating, and contemplating on a daily basis if you're going to hit that vein of gold that holds those inspirations that are yours to act upon. If you're not cultivating a consistent connection with your creativity and with Source, you run the risk of running dry and out of ideas causing you to scramble to try to force something into play.

That never works.

This Full Moon invites you to ask yourself what you need to do to establish a consistent and strong creative practice that allows you to commune daily with your Muse.

CONTEMPLATIONS:

◊ What needs to be healed, released, aligned and brought to my awareness for me to establish a consistent and clear connection with my creativity?

◊ What blocks and limitations do I need to remove so that I can have a clear and strong connection with my creative Muse?

◊ What do I need to release and align so that I can stay consistently inspired?

CHALLENGE:

To learn to be a conduit for Divine Inspiration. To be patient and wait for alignment and right timing before taking action. To be at peace with the stewardship of ideas and to learn to trust the divine trajectory of an inspiration.

OPTIMAL EXPRESSION:

The ability to cultivate a deep relationship with the Divine Muse, to nurture the inspirational fruits of the muse, and to serve as a steward for inspiration by aligning the idea energetically and preparing the way by laying foundational action and building.

JULY 10, 2025

FULL MOON

UNBALANCED EXPRESSION:

To react to the pressure that you have to fulfill an inspiration and to use force to push the inspiration into form even though it might not be your idea/dream to manifest or the right time to bring it forth.

AFFIRMATION:

I am a conduit for the Divine. I am here to allow the creative flow of the Cosmos to flow through me and to let inspiration lead my aligned actions. My relationship with my Muse is an essential part of my creative fulfillment. I consistently take the time and create the space I need to train my body and my energy to stay connected to my creativity. I am inspired, and I act on my inspiration in a way that lets the Universe know I'm ready to create!

JULY 13, 2025

GATE 62: PREPARATION

CHALLENGE:

To trust that you will be prepared for the next step. To not let worry and over-preparation distract you from being present in the moment. To let the fear of not being ready keep you trapped.

AFFIRMATION:

I create the foundation for the practice of excellence by engineering the plan of action that creates growth. I am in the flow of my understanding, and I use my knowledge and experience to be prepared for the evolution of what is next. I am ready and I am prepared. I trust my own preparation and allow myself to be in the flow of what is next knowing that I will know what I need to know when I need to know it.

EFT SETUP:

Even though I feel pressure to do something, I now choose to relax and trust the power of my dreams to call the right circumstance to me, and I deeply and completely love and accept myself.

EARTH:

Gate 61: Wonder

This week take some time to look up at the sky. Go somewhere where you can see the stars if possible and gaze at the face of the Cosmos with awe. Bring the feeling of awe into your everyday life.

JOURNAL QUESTIONS:

◊ Do I worry? What do I do to manage my worry?

◊ What can I do to trust that I know what I need to know?

◊ What proof do I have that I am in the flow of preparation?

◊ Is there anything in my life right now that I need to plan for?

◊ Am I over-planning? Does my need for contingency plans keep me stuck?

MERCURY
RETROGRADE CYCLE

July 18 - August 11

July 18 - Gate 7, the Gate of Collaboration
July 26 - Gate 33, the Gate of Re-Telling
August 3 - Gate 31, the Gate of the Leader

Retrograde cycles encourage us to go inward to explore the themes the planets give us. Mercury is the planet associated with communication. When Mercury goes retrograde, it gives us an opportunity to go inward and contemplate how we can better align ourselves to have greater influence and impact in the world. Take your time to find the right words during this cycle. Do your best not to make big decisions, sign contracts, or make large purchases. Expect delays. Breathe and be patient with others (and yourself)!

This Mercury Retrograde cycle highlights the theme of leadership. True leadership comes from the Heart, is collaborative and democratic, and sets a course for a future rooted in personal sovereignty, justice, and equitability. True leaders hold these energies and are recognized and placed in leadership roles.

Leadership is not limiting, overpowering, imperialistic, or dictatorial. It is also not reactive and revengeful, rooted in stories of the past.

This Mercury retrograde cycle's theme is simple and clear. Where do you need to reclaim sovereignty over your story so that you can take back control of your own life, your own trajectory, and the unlimited expression of who you are in the world?

Be prepared for the potential for power struggles. Remember, real leaders will not let the patterns of the past limit them, and they lead with Love.

CONTEMPLATIONS:

◊ What needs to be healed, released, aligned, and brought to your awareness for you to reclaim your power of the story you tell yourself and the world about who you are?

_____

_____

_____

_____

_____

_____

_____

_____

_____

_____

_____

July 18

July 26

August 3

MERCURY
RETROGRADE CYCLE

CHALLENGE:

To reclaim your personal story. To use your personal alignment with your new, empowered narrative as an influential source of power.

OPTIMAL EXPRESSION:

To tell a story of your own choosing about who you are and how you are. To reclaim your story from limiting events of the past so that you are creating an authentic, unlimited identity that supports you in being able to influence the world around you.

UNBALANCED EXPRESSION:

To try to force, usurp, or take resources and power that do not belong to you. To deny your own power by limiting yourself with stories of victimhood and lack.

AFFIRMATION:

I am a powerful, influential leader. I lead first by taking control of my personal story. I tell myself and the world a story about myself as being unlimited. I have transcended the patterns of the past. I am a victor and a leader. I use my sovereignty over myself to lead others to do the same. As we reclaim our personal stories, we build a collective narrative of peace, hope, abundance, sustainability, justice, and, ultimately, love.

July 18

July 26

August 3

JULY 19, 2025
GATE 56: EXPANSION

CHALLENGE:

To learn to share stories and inspirations with the right people at the right time. To learn to tell stories of expansion and not depletion and contraction.

AFFIRMATION:

I am a Divine Storyteller. The stories of possibility that I share have the power to inspire others to grow and expand. I use my words as a template for possibility and expansion for the world. I inspire the world with my words.

EFT SETUP:

Even though I'm afraid to share my ideas, I now choose to take leadership with my inspirations and share my precious ideas with others, and I deeply and completely love and accept myself.

EARTH:

Gate 60: Conservation

Gratitude is the gateway to transformation. This week take stock of everything in your life that IS good and that IS working. Make a daily list of the things you're grateful for.

JOURNAL QUESTIONS:

◊ What stories do I share repeatedly with others?

◊ Do they lift people up or cause them to contract?

◊ What stories do I tell about myself and my voice that cause me to either expand or contract?

◊ What am I here to inspire others to do or be?

JULY 24, 2025

NEW MOON

Leo 2 degrees, 7 minutes

Gate 56: The Gate of Expansion

New Moon energy invites us to explore how we can deepen our alignment with our intentions and asks us to focus on what we want to grow and expand on in our lives.

The stories we tell ourselves and the world about who we are and how we are set the tone and direction for our lives. If you don't like the direction your life is taking you, the first place to start shifting direction is by telling a better story.

This New Moon invites you to explore your personal narrative and gauge whether it's expansive enough to support your growth. Are you telling a story of possibility and potential, or are you allowing tales of limitation and lack to stop you from creating what you truly want?

What new stories do you need to be telling yourself that support your fulfillment and abundance?

CONTEMPLATIONS:

What new stories do you need to write about yourself, your relationship with money, your friendships and partnerships, your creative fulfillment, your work, your lifestyle, and your spiritual connection? Write them down and offer them to the New Moon so she can bless you with expansion and growth!

CHALLENGE:

To learn to share stories and inspirations with the right people at the right time. To learn to tell stories of expansion and not depletion and contraction.

OPTIMAL EXPRESSION:

The ability to share stories and inspirations that stimulate expansive and possibility-oriented thinking in others for the sake of stimulating powerful emotional energy that creates evolution and growth.

UNBALANCED EXPRESSION:

To get lost or stuck in limiting stories and narratives. To tell stories that contract and deplete the energy of others.

JULY 24, 2025

NEW MOON

AFFIRMATION:

The words contained within my story form the energetic template of what's to come. I choose my words and my stories carefully. I tell stories of worthiness, expansion, abundance, possibility, growth and blessings. The stories I tell myself and the world bless me and those who bear witness to them. I am a cosmic storyteller using my words to build a new world.

JULY 25, 2025

GATE 31: THE LEADER

CHALLENGE:

To learn to lead as a representative of the people you are leading. To cultivate a leadership agenda of service. To not let your fear of not being seen, heard, or accepted get in the way of healthy leadership. To learn to take your rightful place as a leader and not hide out.

AFFIRMATION:

I am a natural born leader. I serve at my highest potential when I am empowering others by giving them a voice and then serving their needs. I use my power to lead people to a greater expansion of who they are and to support them in increasing their abundance, sustainability, and peace.

EFT SETUP:

Even though I'm afraid to be seen, I now choose to express myself and the magnificence that is me with gusto, courage, awareness of my own power and preciousness, and I deeply and completely love and accept myself.

JOURNAL QUESTIONS:

◊ How do I feel about being a leader?

◊ Am I comfortable leading?

◊ Do I shrink from taking leadership?

◊ What is my place of service? Who do I serve?

EARTH:

Gate 41: Imagination

Your imagination is one of the most powerful creative tools you have access to. Spend time this week practicing using your imagination. What do you dream of? What other possibilities are there? Use your imagination to "see" other potential realities. You don't have to "do" what you imagine. Just use this power to stimulate creative emotional frequencies of energy.

JULY 31, 2025

GATE 33: RETELLING

CHALLENGE:

To learn to share a personal narrative that reflects your true value and your worth. To share a personal narrative when it serves the intention to serve, improving the direction of others. To share history in an empowering way.

AFFIRMATION:

I am a processor of stories. My gift is my ability to help others find the blessings, the love, and the power from stories of pain. I hold people's secrets and stories and transform them to share when the time is right. The stories I tell change the direction of people's lives. I use the power of stories to increase the power of Heart in the world and to help build a world of Love.

EFT SETUP:

Even though my stories from my past have held me back, I now choose to rewrite the story of my life and tell it the way I choose, with forgiveness, embracing the gifts, and honoring my courage and strength in my story, and I deeply and completely love and accept myself.

JOURNAL QUESTIONS:

◊ What personal narratives am I telling that might be keeping me stuck, feeling like a victim, or feeling unlovable? How can I rewrite these stories?

◊ What listening practices do I have? What can I do to listen better so that I can gauge when it is the right time to share in a powerful way?

EARTH:

Gate 19: Attunement

This week spend some time alone in nature. Really feel how your energy feels in the restful embrace of the natural world. Practice "feeling" the energy of others and then contrasting it with your own energy to better understand how to distinguish your energy from the emotional energy around you.

MONTHLY REFLECTIONS

My wins from last month. How can I grow what I know is already working?

_____

_____

_____

_____

_____

_____

_____

_____

_____

_____

_____

_____

_____

_____

_____

_____

_____

_____

_____

_____

_____

_____

_____

_____

_____

_____

_____

_____

_____

_____

MONTHLY REFLECTIONS

AUGUST

AUGUST

Monday	Tuesday	Wednesday	Thursday
4	5	6	7
11	12	13	14
18	19	20	21
25	26	27	28

Friday	Saturday	Sunday	To-Do & Notes
1	2	3	**To-Do:** ○ ○ ○ ○ ○
8	9	10	○ ○ ○ ○ ○ ○
15	16	17	Notes
22	23	24	**AUGUST 2025** Mo Tu We Th Fr Sa Su 1 2 3 4 5 6 7 8 9 10 11 12 13 14 15 16 17 18 19 20 21 22 23 24 25 26 27 28 29 30 31
29	30	31	**SEPTEMBER 2025** Mo Tu We Th Fr Sa Su 1 2 3 4 5 6 7 8 9 10 11 12 13 14 15 16 17 18 19 20 21 22 23 24 25 26 27 28 29 30

MONTHLY INTENTIONS

Who will I be at the end of this month? Who do I need to be in order to fulfill my intentions for the month? How will I feel? What will my life look like? Write it out.

_____

_____

_____

_____

_____

_____

_____

_____

_____

_____

_____

_____

_____

_____

_____

_____

_____

_____

_____

_____

_____

_____

_____

_____

_____

_____

_____

_____

MONTHLY INTENTIONS

What key actions do I need to take to make the fulfillment of my intentions for this month my reality by the end of the month?

_____
_____
_____
_____
_____
_____
_____
_____
_____
_____
_____
_____
_____
_____
_____
_____
_____
_____
_____
_____
_____
_____
_____
_____
_____
_____

MONTHLY READING

Using divination cards of your choice, pull three cards to help you set your intentions for the month.
Get your own Quantum Cards at: **https://quantumhumandesign.com/quantum-cards**

CARD 1

What influences and lessons from the past need to be mastered to support my evolution?

_____

_____

_____

_____

_____

_____

CARD 2

What is my overarching theme this month that I need to pay attention to? What lessons does this card bring me?

_____

_____

_____

_____

_____

_____

CARD 3

What do I need to strengthen and master to move forward?

_____

_____

_____

_____

_____

_____

AUGUST 5, 2025

GATE 7: COLLABORATION

CHALLENGE:

To understand the need to be in front and allow yourself to serve through building teams, collaborating, and influencing the figurehead of leadership. To be at peace with serving the leader through support and collaboration. To recognize that the voice of the leader is only as strong and powerful as the support he/she receives.

AFFIRMATION:

I am an agent of peace who influences the direction and organization of leadership. I unify people around ideas. I influence with my wisdom, my knowledge, and my connections. I am a team builder, a collaborator, and I organize people in ways that empower them and support them in creating a collective direction rooted in compassion.

EFT SETUP:

Even though I feel confused and conflicted about what to do, I trust the Divine Flow and let the Universe show me the right thing to do in the right time, and I deeply and completely love, trust, and accept myself.

JOURNAL QUESTIONS:

◊ What are my gifts and strengths? How do I use those gifts to influence and lead others?

◊ How do I feel about not being the figurehead of leadership?

◊ What happens when I only support the leadership? Do I still feel powerful? Influential?

◊ Make a list of the times when my influence has positively directed leadership.

EARTH:

Gate 13: Narrative

Take some time this week to really listen to the story you're telling about who you are. Is it big enough? Are you taking control of your own story or are you allowing the past to define who you are? If you were going to rewrite your story, what would you say about yourself? How can you make your personal narrative more true to who you really are?

AUGUST 9, 2025

FULL MOON

Forgiveness is not about what happened. It's about taking back control of the narrative. This Full Moon invites you to reclaim sovereignty over any narrative that has caused you to feel disempowered or like a victim. How can you rewrite the narrative so that you emerge with a lesson that makes you stronger or in such a way that you become the victor, not the victim?

Aquarius 16 degrees, 59 minutes

Gate 13: The Gate of Narrative

Full moon energy invites us to explore what we need to release and let go of in order to stay in alignment with our intentions.

Forgiveness is not about forgetting or even condoning what someone has done to you. Forgiveness is about reclaiming your part of the story from an event that may have left you feeling powerless or like a victim. If you don't reclaim your own narrative from the event, you run the risk of staying stuck in a story of lack and victimhood.

Research shows that when you intentionally rewrite the story of a past painful event in such a way that you emerge from the story with a powerful lesson that makes you stronger or as the victor of the story instead of the victim, you strengthen your health and your well-being. You can rewrite your story in any way you choose, even in a fantastical way! (The brain doesn't know the difference!).

CONTEMPLATIONS:

◊ What is the TRUE story of who you are? Did you forget about your beauty, your power, your strength, your courage, your capability, your creativity? What new story can you tell that includes the TRUTH about who you are? (Hint: You are an infinitely powerful, creative, amazing force in this world who came here to make this world an even more beautiful and better place! Thank you for being YOU!)

_____

_____

_____

_____

_____

_____

_____

_____

_____

_____

_____

_____

_____

CHALLENGE:

To forgive the past and redefine who you are each and every day. To tell a personal narrative that is empowering, self-loving, and reflects your value and your authentic self. To bear witness to the pain and narrative of others and offer them a better story that allows them to expand on their abundance and blessings.

OPTIMAL EXPRESSION:

The ability to use the power of personal narrative to create with power and intention.

UNBALANCED EXPRESSION:

Staying stuck in old stories. Holding on to old past pains. Staying the victim in a story that repeats itself because your personal narrative is stuck in an old story.

285

AUGUST 9, 2025

FULL MOON

AFFIRMATION:

I am the only person in the world with the power and permission to tell the story of Who I Am. I am who I declare myself to be, and I am sovereign over the story I tell myself and the world about who I am and how I am. I am powerful. I am a victor, and I reclaim my power, my value, my love, and my worthiness from any limiting narrative I may be telling about myself. My capacity to tell my own story is the immutable source of my creative power.

AUGUST 11, 2025

CHALLENGE:

To learn to embrace ideas as possibilities, not answers, and to let the power of the possibility stimulate the imagination as a way of calibrating the emotions and the Heart. This Gate teaches us the power of learning to wait to see which possibility actually manifests in the physical world and to experiment with options in response.

AFFIRMATION:

I am tuned into the cosmic flow of possibility. I am inspired about exploring new possibilities and potentials. I use the power of my thoughts to stretch the limits of what is known and engage my imagination to explore the potential of the unknown.

EFT SETUP:

Even though I don't know what to do, I allow my questions to seed the Universe and I trust and wait with great patience that the answers will be revealed to me, and I deeply and completely love and accept myself.

JOURNAL QUESTIONS:

◊ What ideas do I have right now that need me to nurture and activate them?

◊ What possibilities do these ideas stimulate right now? Take some time to write or visualize the possibilities.

◊ Am I comfortable with waiting? What can I do to increase my patience and curiosity?

EARTH:

Gate 49: The Catalyst

Are you holding onto a situation for too long? Do you have a habit of quitting too soon? Is there a circumstance or condition in your life that you are allowing or running from because you fear the emotional energy associated with change? What needs to be healed or released?

AUGUST 17, 2025

GATE 29: DEVOTION

CHALLENGE:

To discover what and who you need to devote yourself to. To sustain yourself so that you can sustain your devotion. To learn to say no to what you need to say no to and to learn to say yes to what you want to say yes to.

AFFIRMATION:

I have an extraordinary ability to devote myself to the manifestation of an idea. My commitment to my story and to the fulfillment of my intention changes the story of what is possible in my own life and for humanity. I choose my commitments with great care. I devote myself to what is vital for the evolution of the world, and I nurture myself first because my wellbeing is the foundation of what I create.

EFT SETUP:

Even though I am afraid to invest all my effort into my dream. What if it fails? What if I'm crazy? What if I just need to buckle down and be "normal?" I choose to do it anyway. I deeply, and completely, love and accept myself.

EARTH:

Gate 30: Passion

What do you need to do this week to sustain your vision or dream about what you are inspired to create in your life?

JOURNAL QUESTIONS:

◊ What devotion do I have right now that drives me?

◊ Is this a devotion that inspires me, or do I feel overly obligated to it?

◊ Who would I be and what would I choose if I gave myself permission to say no more often?

◊ What would I like to say no to that I am saying yes to right now?

◊ What obligations do I need to take off my plate right now?

◊ What would I like to devote myself to?

AUGUST 23, 2025

GATE 59: SUSTAINABILITY

CHALLENGE:

To learn to make abundant choices that sustain you, and at the same time, others. To collaborate and initiate others into sustainable relationships from a place of sufficiency. To learn to share what you have in a sustainable way.

AFFIRMATION:

The energy I carry has the power to create sufficiency and sustainability for all. I craft valuable alliances and agreements that support me in expanding abundance for everyone. I hold to higher principles and values that are rooted in my trust in sufficiency and the all-providing Source. Through my work and alignments my blessings serve to increase the blessings of myself and others.

EFT SETUP:

Even though I struggle to share my intentions, I now choose to state them boldly and wait for the pieces of my creation to magically fall into place, and I deeply and completely love and accept myself.

EARTH:

Gate 55: Faith

This week, deepen your experience of beauty. Surround yourself with beauty. Consciously bring beauty into your daily life and notice how abundantly beautiful life truly is.

JOURNAL QUESTIONS:

◊ Do I trust in my own abundance?

◊ How do I feel about sharing what I have with others?

◊ Am I creating relationship and partnership agreements that honor my work?

◊ Do I have relationships and agreements that are draining me? What needs to change?

◊ How do I feel about being "right?"

◊ Am I open to other ways of thinking or being?

◊ Do I believe in creating agreements and alignments with people who have different values and perspectives?

AUGUST 23, 2025

NEW MOON

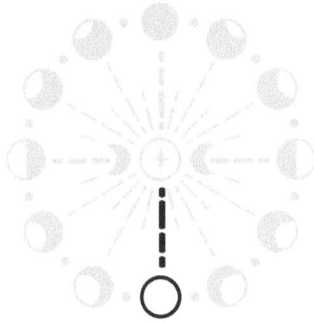

Virgo 0 degrees, 22 minutes

Gate 59: The Gate of Sustainability

New Moon energy invites us to explore how we can deepen our alignment with our intentions and asks us to focus on what we want to grow and expand on in our lives.

Earlier this year we worked deeply with the Gate 6, the Gate of Impact and the electromagnetic to the Gate 59. Both of these energies bring us the theme of working and creating resources to share with our families, our loved ones and our communities. This work can not be done if it's not done sustainably, otherwise we run the risk of boom and bust cycles of energy and resources, leading to lack and scarcity.

This New Moon invites us to explore what key actions need to be taken to create support and fulfillment in your life. Are your actions producing the results that you are seeking? If not, what needs to be strengthened so that you can optimize your energy and your actions?

This is a new invitation to explore whether you can simplify what you're doing or even let go of some of your busy-ness. Often this calls for some soul-searching and reprioritizing so that you're most effective with your work. When we trust that we can have enough, it can often lead to relaxing and allowing more to flow in.

Another aspect of this energy is about relationship energy. In particular, this Gate regulates sex and sexuality. Make sure that you're taking time to connect with your partner and cultivate the presence necessary to create true intimacy.

CONTEMPLATIONS:

◊ Take stock of how you're spending your time. Does your time reflect your priorities? What needs to shift?

◊ What new key actions do you need to take to produce more results with less effort?

◊ What new patterns and habits do you need to establish to create more time for genuine intimacy and connection in your life?

_____

_____

_____

_____

_____

_____

_____

_____

_____

_____

CHALLENGE:

To learn to make abundant choices that sustain you and, at the same time, others. To collaborate and initiate others into sustainable relationships from a place of sufficiency. To learn to share what you have in a sustainable way.

OPTIMAL EXPRESSION:

To trust in sufficiency and to know that when you create abundance, there is great fulfillment in sharing. To craft partnerships and relationships that sustain you and the foundation of your life.

UNBALANCED EXPRESSION:

To feel like you have to fight or struggle to survive. To feel the need to penetrate others and force your "rightness" on them. To let fear of lack cause you to craft unsustainable relationships and agreements.

AUGUST 23, 2025

NEW MOON

AFFIRMATION:

When I am aligned with the energy of my abundance and I trust that I have all that I need, I make good, strong choices about how I use my energy and my effort. I simplify and clarify regularly to make sure that I am doing exactly what needs to be done and I conserve my energy in order to be more present to those I love and to myself. When I trust in my support I access more abundant and expansive ideas and I create with confidence.

AUGUST 29, 2025

GATE 40: RESTORATION

CHALLENGE:

To learn to value yourself enough to retreat from community and the energy of those you love to restore, restock, and replenish your inner resources. To learn to interpret the signal of loneliness correctly. To take responsibility for your own care and resources and to not abdicate your own power to take care of yourself.

AFFIRMATION:

I am a powerful resource for my community. The energy that I hold impacts others deeply and brings them to deeper states of alignment and sustainability. I take care of my body, mind, and soul because I know the more that I am and the more that I have, the more I can give to others. I take care of myself first because I know that good things flow from me. I am valuable and powerful, and I claim and defend the true story of Who I Truly Am.

EFT SETUP:

Even though it is hard to let go of the obligations of relationships, I now choose to release all relationships that are draining and unsupportive, and I deeply and completely love and accept myself.

JOURNAL QUESTIONS:

◊ What role does loneliness play in my life?

◊ Has loneliness caused me to doubt my value?

◊ What do I need to do to restore my energy?

◊ Am I doing enough to take care of myself?

◊ What agreements am I making in my relationships that might be causing me to compromise my value?

◊ How can I rewrite these agreements?

◊ Am I abdicating my responsibility for my self-care?

◊ Am I living a "martyr" model?

◊ What needs to be healed, released, aligned, and brought to my awareness for me to take responsibility for cultivating my own sense of value and my self-worth?

EARTH:

Gate 37: Peace

When you feel that your outer world is chaotic and disrupted, how do you cultivate inner peace? Practice anchoring yourself in deep inner peace this week.

MONTHLY REFLECTIONS

My wins from last month. How can I grow what I know is already working?

_____
_____
_____
_____
_____
_____
_____
_____
_____
_____
_____
_____
_____
_____
_____
_____
_____
_____
_____
_____
_____
_____
_____
_____
_____
_____
_____
_____

MONTHLY REFLECTIONS

SEPTEMBER

SEPTEMBER

Monday	Tuesday	Wednesday	Thursday
1	2	3	4
8	9	10	11
15	16	17	18
22	23	24	25
29	30		

Friday	Saturday	Sunday	To-Do & Notes
5	6	7	**To-Do:**
			○
			○
			○
			○
			○
12	13	14	○
			○
			○
			○
			○
			○
19	20	21	Notes
26	27	28	

SEPTEMBER 2025

Mo	Tu	We	Th	Fr	Sa	Su
1	2	3	4	5	6	7
8	9	10	11	12	13	14
15	16	17	18	19	20	21
22	23	24	25	26	27	28
29	30					

OCTOBER 2025

Mo	Tu	We	Th	Fr	Sa	Su
		1	2	3	4	5
6	7	8	9	10	11	12
13	14	15	16	17	18	19
20	21	22	23	24	25	26
27	28	29	30	31		

MONTHLY INTENTIONS

Who will I be at the end of this month? Who do I need to be in order to fulfill my intentions for the month? How will I feel? What will my life look like? Write it out.

_____

_____

_____

_____

_____

_____

_____

_____

_____

_____

_____

_____

_____

_____

_____

_____

_____

_____

_____

_____

_____

_____

_____

_____

_____

_____

_____

_____

_____

MONTHLY INTENTIONS

What key actions do I need to take to make the fulfillment of my intentions for this month my reality by the end of the month?

_____

_____

_____

_____

_____

_____

_____

_____

_____

_____

_____

_____

_____

_____

_____

_____

_____

_____

_____

_____

_____

_____

_____

_____

_____

_____

_____

_____

MONTHLY READING

Using divination cards of your choice, pull three cards to help you set your intentions for the month.
Get your own Quantum Cards at: **https://quantumhumandesign.com/quantum-cards**

CARD 1

What influences and lessons from the past need to be mastered to support my evolution?

_____

_____

_____

_____

_____

_____

CARD 2

What is my overarching theme this month that I need to pay attention to? What lessons does this card bring me?

_____

_____

_____

_____

_____

_____

CARD 3

What do I need to strengthen and master to move forward?

_____

_____

_____

_____

_____

_____

_____

CONTEMPLATIONS

SEPTEMBER 4, 2025

GATE 64: DIVINE TRANSFERENCE

CHALLENGE:

To not let the power of your big ideas overwhelm you and shut down your dreaming and creating. Do not get lost in the pressure of answering the how question.

AFFIRMATION:

I am a conduit for expansive thinking. My inspirations and ideas create the seeds of possibility in my mind and in the mind of others. I honor the dreams that pass through my mind and allow my big ideas to stimulate my imagination and the imagination of others. I trust the Universe to reveal the details of my dreams when the time is right. I use the power of my dreams to stimulate a world of possibility and expansion.

EFT SETUP:

Even though I don't know what is next, I wait and trust that the perfect right step will show up for me, and I deeply and completely love and accept myself.

Even though I feel overwhelmed with ideas, I trust the Universe to reveal the next step to me. I relax and wait, and I deeply and completely love and accept myself.

JOURNAL QUESTIONS:

◊ What do I do to take care of my Big Ideas?

◊ How do I feel about having dreams but not always the solutions?

◊ How can I stop judging the gift of my dreams?

◊ Do I trust that the how of my ideas will be revealed?

◊ How can I deepen this trust?

EARTH:

Gate 63: Curiosity

What needs to happen to unlock your attachment to being "right" and to allow yourself to dream of other possibilities? What if there's more than what you can see right now...?

SEPTEMBER 7, 2025
FULL MOON/TOTAL LUNAR ECLIPSE

This Full Moon invites you to explore what you need to release and cultivate in order to see the world through the creative lens of curiosity and wonder.

CONTEMPLATIONS:

◊ What needs to be healed, released, aligned and brought to your awareness for you to see the world with an open and curious mind?

◊ What do you need to do to stimulate your curiosity and your creativity?

Pisces 15 degrees, 24 minutes
Gate 63: The Gate of Curiosity

Full moon energy invites us to explore what we need to release and let go of to stay in alignment with our intentions. Eclipse energy amplifies the moon's energy. This moon offers us a powerful push to release and let go of old limitations and stuckness.

Curiosity breeds imagination. Your imagination creates neurotransmitters which, in turn, create emotions and vibrational frequencies which program your body into a highly coherent state of creativity (or not - depending on the emotions generated). When we cultivate curiosity, we amplify our creativity.

The shadow of this energy is self-doubt and doubt in general. If you set out exploring the world with curiosity and you're simultaneously doubting the world or yourself, you're effectively shutting down your creative power and limiting yourself to continuing to choose options from the same box you've been choosing from all your life.

CHALLENGE:

To not let self-doubt and suspicion cause you to stop being curious.

OPTIMAL EXPRESSION:

The ability to use questioning and curiosity as a way of stimulating dreams of new possibilities and potentials. Thoughts that inspire the question of what needs to happen to make an idea a reality.

UNBALANCED EXPRESSION:

Doubt (especially self-doubt) that leads to suspicion and the struggle for certainty. The unwillingness to question an old idea. The loss of curiosity.

SEPTEMBER 7, 2025

FULL MOON/TOTAL LUNAR ECLIPSE

AFFIRMATION:

I see the world with curious eyes.
I ask questions. I wonder. I am
in awe. I imagine solutions to my
challenges and allow my mind to
expand with the possibility of new
solutions to old challenges. I am
open-minded and explore new ideas
with hunger and the willingness to
explore new frontiers of knowing
and thinking.

SEPTEMBER 9, 2025

GATE 47: MINDSET

CHALLENGE:

To become skilled at a mindset of open-ness and possibility. Do not let inspiration die because you don't know how to fulfill it.

AFFIRMATION:

My mindset is the source of my inspired actions and attitude. I know that when I receive an idea and inspiration it is my job to nurture the idea by using the power of my imagination to increase the potential and emotional frequency of the idea. I consistently keep my inner and outer environment aligned with the energy of possibility and potential. I know that it is my job to create by virtue of my alignment, and I relax knowing that it is the job of the Universe to fulfill my inspirations.

EFT SETUP:

Even though it is frustrating to not know how to make something happen, I now choose to wait for Divine Insight, and I trust that the right information will be revealed to me at the perfect time, and I deeply and completely love and accept myself.

EARTH:

Gate 22: Surrender

Where are you denying your passion in your life? What is one thing you can do this week to reclaim your passion?

JOURNAL QUESTIONS:

◊ What thoughts do I have when I receive an idea or inspiration?

◊ Am I hopeful or despairing?

◊ How does it feel to let go of figuring out how I'm going to make my idea a reality?

◊ What do I do to regulate my mindset?

◊ What practices do I need to cultivate to increase the power of my thoughts?

SEPTEMBER 15, 2025

GATE 6: IMPACT

CHALLENGE:

To become proficient in using emotional energy and learn to trust that your impact is in service to the world. When you understand that your life is a vehicle for service and your energy is being used to influence and impact those around you, you assume greater obligation and responsibility to maintain a high frequency of energy. The quality of the emotional energy you cultivate influences others to come together in an equitable, sustainable, and peaceful way. Learning to trust that your words and impact will have effect when the timing is correct and not overriding Divine Timing.

AFFIRMATION:

My emotional energy influences the world around me. I am rooted in the energy of equity, sustainability, and peace. When I am aligned with abundance, I am an energetic source of influence that facilitates elegant solutions to creating peace and wellbeing. I am deliberate and aligned with values that create peace in my life, in my community, and in the world.

JOURNAL QUESTIONS:

◊ What do I need to do to deepen my trust in Divine Timing?

◊ What do I need to do to prepare myself to be seen and to have influence?

◊ What do I need to do to sustain my emotional energy in order to align with peaceful and sustainable solutions?

◊ How do I feel about lack? How do I feel about abundance? How can I create a greater degree of emotional abundance in my life? In my daily practice?

EFT SETUP:

Even though I am ready to leap into action, I now choose to take a breath, wait out my emotions, and trust that the right timing will be revealed to me. I'm not missing out on anything. Divine Order is the rule of the day, and I deeply and completely love and accept myself.

EARTH:

Gate 36: Exploration

Go on a "miracle hunt" today. Make a list of all the unexpected synchronous and serendipitous events that have happened in your life. What has been the greatest miracle or unexpected event you've experienced in your life?

SEPTEMBER 21, 2025

GATE 46: EMBODIMENT

CHALLENGE:

To learn to love your body. To learn to fully be in your body. To learn to love the sensual nature of your physical form and to move it with love and awareness.

AFFIRMATION:

My body is the vehicle for my soul. My ability to fully express who I am (and my life and soul purpose) is deeply rooted in my body's ability to carry my soul. I love, nurture, and commit to my body. I appreciate all of its miraculous abilities and form. Every day I love my body more.

EFT SETUP:

Even though it is hard for me to love my body, I now choose to embrace my amazing physical form and honor it for all the good it brings me, and I deeply and completely love and accept myself.

EARTH:

Gate 25: Spirit

Do you have a regular practice that connects you to Source? How can you deepen this practice this week?

JOURNAL QUESTIONS:

◊   Do I love my body?

◊   What can I do to deepen my love for my body?

◊   What parts of my body do I love and appreciate?

◊   Make a list of every part of my body that I love.

◊   What do I need to do to amplify the Life Force I am experiencing in my body?

◊   What kinds of devotion and commitment do I experience that help me harness greater amounts of Life Force in my body?

◊   How can I deepen my commitment and devotion to my body?

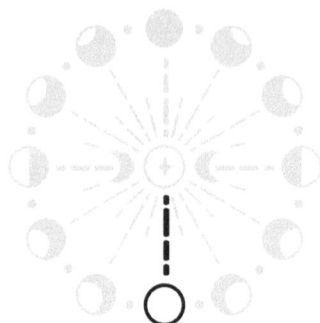

Virgo 28 degrees, 59 minutes

Gate 46: The Gate of Embodiment

New Moon energy invites us to explore how we can deepen our alignment with our intentions and asks us to focus on what we want to grow and expand on in our lives. Eclipse energy amplifies the theme of the New Moon.

As we tumble through this year exploring the relationship between our higher purpose, our personal will and well-being, and how we can influence our collective direction and our connection to community with our unique and important individual lives, the moon pulls us back and reminds us we can do nothing without the health and well-being of the body.

With the eclipse amping up this theme we are encouraged to explore the quality of our physical energy and our health. This New Moon is practical and reminds us that momentum must be built on a foundation of health and vitality. Burnout makes it very difficult to move forward.

There's a chicken and egg thing happening here with this energy. Alignment with our purpose and our authentic selves AND healing our self-worth makes it much easier to tap into our vitality and energy. And, with all of the uncertainty, tension and disruption in this year, it's been pretty easy to neglect our bodies, making us vulnerable to burnout and even "ego depletion" that happens with physical exhaustion.

This powerful New Moon reminds us to care for ourselves and our bodies. We can't simply think and dream; we also have to move and groove and resist the seduction of inertia. This is a time to start (or restart) a practice that allows you to fully be present and embody your body. No more going through the motions, but rather, really dropping in and leaning into the message your body has for you and creating a deep and loving relationship with your physical form.

(Maybe dance under the moon a bit tonight!)

CONTEMPLATIONS:

◊ What does your body need to feel vital and alive?

◊ What practices do you need to cultivate to keep your body feeling vital and vibrating?

CHALLENGE:

To learn to love your body. To learn to fully be in your body. To learn to love the sensual nature of your physical form and to move it with love and awareness.

OPTIMAL EXPRESSION:

To recognize that the body is the vehicle for the soul and to love the body as a vital element of the soul's expression in life. To nurture, be grounded in, and fully care for the body. To savor the physicality of the human experience. To explore how to fully embody the spirit in your body and to be committed and devoted to seeing how much life force you can embody into your physical form.

SEPTEMBER 21, 2025
NEW MOON/PARTIAL SOLAR ECLIPSE

UNBALANCED EXPRESSION:

To disconnect from the body. To
hate the body. To avoid nurturing
or taking care of the body. To avoid
the commitments and consistency
necessary to fully embody life force.
To hide or disfigure the body.

AFFIRMATION:

My body is a precious vehicle for
my soul. I love, honor, nurture, and
nourish my body, feeding it with
good energy, food, and movement
to keep it vital and healthy. I take
time to listen and connect with my
body's wisdom, knowing that my
body holds vital cues and clues to
help me know what's right for me.
I support my body in releasing that
which no longer serves it and move
it with joy and delight.

SEPTEMBER 27, 2025

GATE 18: RE-ALIGNMENT

CHALLENGE:

To learn to wait for the right timing and the right circumstances to offer your intuitive insights into how to fix or correct a pattern. To wait for the right time and the right reason to share your critique. To understand that the purpose of re-alignment is to create more joy, not to be "right."

AFFIRMATION:

I am a powerful force that re-aligns patterns. My insights and awareness give people the information they need to deepen their expertise and experience greater joy. I serve joy, and I align the patterns of the world to increase the world's potential for living in the flow of joy.

EFT SETUP:

Even though I feel criticized and judged, I now choose to hear the wisdom of the correction and release my personal attachment, and I deeply and completely love and accept myself.

EARTH:

Gate 17: Anticipation

What do you need to do to release any doubts and fears you may have about your own ability? What accomplishments do you have that you can celebrate and acknowledge?

JOURNAL QUESTIONS:

◊ What does joy mean to me? How do I serve it? How do I cultivate joy in my own life?

◊ How does it feel to be "right" about something and keep it to myself?

◊ Do I need to release any old stories about needing to be right?

◊ Do I trust my own insights? Do I have the courage to share them when it is necessary?

MONTHLY REFLECTIONS

My wins from last month. How can I grow what I know is already working?

_____
_____
_____
_____
_____
_____
_____
_____
_____
_____
_____
_____
_____
_____
_____
_____
_____
_____
_____
_____
_____
_____
_____
_____
_____
_____
_____
_____

MONTHLY REFLECTIONS

OCTOBER

OCTOBER

Monday	Tuesday	Wednesday	Thursday
		1	2
6	7	8	9
13	14	15	16
20	21	22	23
27	28	29	30

Friday	Saturday	Sunday	To-Do & Notes
3	4	5	**To-Do:** ○ ○ ○ ○ ○
10	11	12	○ ○ ○ ○ ○ ○
17	18	19	Notes
24	25	26	
31			

OCTOBER 2025

Mo	Tu	We	Th	Fr	Sa	Su
		1	2	3	4	5
6	7	8	9	10	11	12
13	14	15	16	17	18	19
20	21	22	23	24	25	26
27	28	29	30	31		

NOVEMBER 2025

Mo	Tu	We	Th	Fr	Sa	Su
					1	2
3	4	5	6	7	8	9
10	11	12	13	14	15	16
17	18	19	20	21	22	23
24	25	26	27	28	29	30

MONTHLY INTENTIONS

Who will I be at the end of this month? Who do I need to be in order to fulfill my intentions for the month? How will I feel? What will my life look like? Write it out.

_____

_____

_____

_____

_____

_____

_____

_____

_____

_____

_____

_____

_____

_____

_____

_____

_____

_____

_____

_____

_____

_____

_____

_____

_____

_____

_____

_____

_____

MONTHLY INTENTIONS

What key actions do I need to take to make the fulfillment of my intentions for this month my reality by the end of the month?

_____

_____

_____

_____

_____

_____

_____

_____

_____

_____

_____

_____

_____

_____

_____

_____

_____

_____

_____

_____

_____

_____

_____

_____

_____

_____

MONTHLY READING

Using divination cards of your choice, pull three cards to help you set your intentions for the month.
Get your own Quantum Cards at: **https://quantumhumandesign.com/quantum-cards**

CARD 1

What influences and lessons from the past need to be mastered to support my evolution?

_____

_____

_____

_____

_____

_____

CARD 2

What is my overarching theme this month that I need to pay attention to? What lessons does this card bring me?

_____

_____

_____

_____

_____

_____

CARD 3

What do I need to strengthen and master to move forward?

_____

_____

_____

_____

_____

_____

_____

OCTOBER 2, 2025

GATE 48: WISDOM

CHALLENGE:

To allow yourself to trust that you will know what you need to know when you need to know it. To not let the fear of not knowing stop you from creating. Do not let not knowing hold you back.

AFFIRMATION:

I am a depth of wisdom and knowledge. My studies and experiences have taught me everything I need to know. I push beyond the limits of my earthly knowledge and take great leaps of faith as a function of my deep connection to Source knowing that I will always know what I need to know when I need to know it.

EFT SETUP:

Even though I am afraid I am not ready to, I now choose to courageously dive in and just do it, and I deeply and completely love and accept myself.

EARTH:

Gate 21: Self-Regulation

How can you be more generous with yourself this week? How can you create an inner and outer environment that is more self-generous?

JOURNAL QUESTIONS:

◊   Do I trust my own knowing?

◊   What needs to be healed, released, aligned, and brought to my awareness for me to deepen my self-trust?

◊   What practice do I have that keeps me connected to the wisdom of Source?

◊   How can I deepen my connection to Source?

OCTOBER 7, 2025

FULL MOON

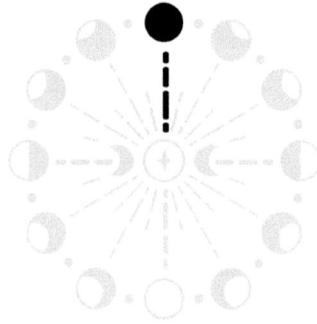

Aries 14 degrees, 8 minutes

Gate 21: The Gate of Self-Regulation

Full moon energy invites us to explore what we need to release and let go of in order to stay in alignment with our intentions.

This Full Moon highlights the theme of self-regulation, self-control and will power. We think that will power is something we simply "have", but research shows that will power can be trained and can be sustainable.

People who take pride in themselves - WHO they are - have sustainable will power. In other words, if you have high self-worth and your personal narrative is a narrative that includes an inner awareness of your inherent value, then you gain access to a better quality of energy.

When we are motivated to do something to prove our value because our inner story of self-worth isn't strong, then we are misaligned and out of integrity with our actions. This misalignment costs vital energy and can, ultimately, lead to burnout.

Willpower is not the source of energy or the driver of your motivation. Self-worth is your source of energy and the driver for your motivation. You do something because it lines up with your value or you have a deep inner knowing that you DESERVE to do it.

You deserve to be wealthy.

You deserve to be healthy.

You deserve to rest and play.

You deserve to fulfill yourself.

If you recoil at the word "deserve," I gently encourage you to use this moon to explore why the idea of "deserving" bothers you. You DO deserve A LOT. What new story do you need to write about your value?

CONTEMPLATIONS:

◊ What needs to be healed, released, aligned, and brought to my awareness so that I can activate sustainable willpower?

◊ What parts of your self-worth story do you need to rewrite?

◊ What do you need to let go of control over?

◊ Where do you need to practice better self-regulation?

CHALLENGE:

To learn to let go. To master self-regulation. To release the need to control others and circumstances. To trust in the Divine and to know that you are supported. Knowing that you are worthy of support and you don't have to over-compensate.

OPTIMAL EXPRESSION:

The ability to regulate your inner and outer environment in order to sustain a vibrational frequency that reflects your true value. The ability to be self-generous and to set boundaries that maintain your value and support you in being sustainable in the world. To take the actions necessary to honor your unique role in the cosmic plan.

OCTOBER 7, 2025

FULL MOON

UNBALANCED EXPRESSION:

To feel the need to control life, others, resources, etc., out of fear that you aren't worthy of being supported.

AFFIRMATION:

I am inherently valuable simply because I exist. There is nothing I have to do to prove my value. I nurture, nourish, and take care of myself and my resources because I deserve to be taken care of. I create an inner and outer environment that reflects my value. I have daily practices that sustain my wellness and well-being. I am fully resourced so that I can intentionally create the life I deserve.

OCTOBER 8, 2025

GATE 57: INSTINCT

CHALLENGE:

To learn to trust your own insights and gut. To learn to tell the difference between an instinctive response versus a fear of the future. To become skilled at your connection to your sense of right timing.

AFFIRMATION:

My Inner Wisdom is deeply connected to the pulse of Divine Timing. I listen to my Inner Wisdom and follow my instincts. I know when and how to prepare for the future. I take guided action and I trust myself and Source.

EFT SETUP:

Even though it is scary to trust my gut, I now choose to honor my awareness, quiet my mind, and go with what feels right, and I deeply and completely love and accept myself.

EARTH:

Gate 51: Initiation

What lessons have unexpected events brought into your life? Make note of how resilient you are...

JOURNAL QUESTIONS:

◊ Do I trust my intuition?

◊ What does my intuition feel like to me?

◊ Sometimes doing a retrospective analysis of my intuition/instinct makes it more clear how my intuitive signal works. What experiences in the past have I had that I knew I should or shouldn't do?

◊ How have I experienced my intuition in the past?

◊ When I think about moving forward in my life, do I feel afraid?

◊ What am I afraid of? What can I do to mitigate the fear?

◊ What impulses am I experiencing that are telling me to prepare for what is next in my life?

◊ Am I acting on my impulses? Why or why not?

OCTOBER 14, 2025

CHALLENGE:

To trust in Divine Timing. To prepare for the next step of manifestation and to align with the unfolding of the process. To be patient.

AFFIRMATION:

I am a Divine translator for Divine Inspiration. I sense and know what needs to be prepared on the earthly plane in order to be ready for right timing. I am aligned with right timing, and I prepare and wait patiently knowing that when the time is right, I am ready to do the work to help transform pain into power.

EFT SETUP:

Even though I have worked hard to make my dreams come true and nothing has happened yet, I trust in Divine Timing and keep tending to my vision, and I deeply and completely love and accept myself.

EARTH:

Gate 42: Conclusion

To get the most out of this week, explore what unfinished business you need to bring to a conclusion. Are there things you need to say? Situations you need to end and be done with? Endings make room for new beginnings...

JOURNAL QUESTIONS:

◊ What do I need to do to be prepared to manifest my vision?

◊ What actionable steps need to be completed in order for me to be ready when the timing is right?

◊ What do I need to do to cultivate patience?

◊ Do I have a fear of failing that is causing me to avoid being prepared?

◊ Am I over-doing and being overly prepared?

◊ Am I pushing too hard?

◊ What can I let go of?

OCTOBER 20, 2025

GATE 50: NURTURING

CHALLENGE:

To transcend guilt and unhealthy obligation and do what you need to do to take care of yourself in order to better serve others. To hold rigid principles to judge others.

AFFIRMATION:

My presence brings Love into the room. I nurture and love others. I take care of myself first in order to be better able to serve Love. I intuitively know what people need and I facilitate for them a state of self-love and self-empowerment by helping them align more deeply with the power of Love. I let go and I allow others to learn from what I model and teach. I am a deep well of love that sustains the planet.

EFT SETUP:

Even though it is hard for me to give and receive love, I now choose to be completely open to receiving and sharing deep and unconditional love starting by deeply and completely loving and accepting myself first.

EARTH:

Gate 3: Innovation

What IS working in your life? Take some time to contemplate what aspects of your current reality you'd love to grow and expand upon.

JOURNAL QUESTIONS:

◊ How do I feel about taking care of myself first?

◊ How do I sustain my nurturing energy?

◊ What role does guilt play in driving and/or motivating me?

◊ What would I choose if I could remove the guilt?

◊ Do I have non-negotiable values? What are they?

◊ How do I handle people who share different values from me?

OCTOBER 21, 2025

NEW MOON

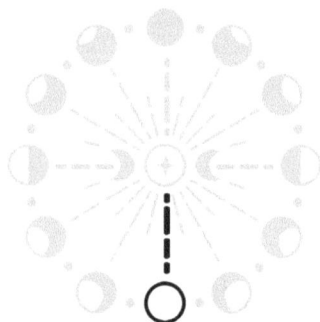

Libra 28 degrees, 21 minutes

Gate 50: The Gate of Nurturing

New Moon energy invites us to explore how we can deepen our alignment with our intentions and asks us to focus on what we want to grow and expand on in our lives.

This New Moon once again turns her attention to relationships, and even though it might feel like you're dealing with your relationship with others, you're actually dealing with your relationship with yourself! The Gate 50 holds the energy for responsibility and asks us to be responsible for the care and teaching of others.

This energy, in the shadow, can bring guilt and fear of failing our responsibility to others. When we work with this energy, we can easily be manipulated by guilt and take on responsibility for things we aren't actually responsible for.

Even though this is New Moon energy, before you can start with a new commitment to nurture yourself so that you can better nurture others, you must start first with an exploration of what (or who) are you feeling responsible for. Are you being responsible for something that isn't yours to be responsible for? If so, time to let it go!

You can not dig deep and give to others if your own bowl is empty. Martyrdom leads to codependency and love with conditions. To love better and to be able to give more, you must take responsibility for yourself first.

Remember, teaching a person to fish rather than feeding them empowers them for a lifetime. Where do you need to teach people to fish?

CONTEMPLATIONS:

◊ What responsibilities do you need to give up?

◊ What responsibilities for yourself have you neglected? What do you need to do to nurture yourself better?

_____

_____

_____

_____

_____

_____

_____

_____

_____

_____

_____

_____

_____

_____

_____

_____

_____

_____

_____

_____

_____

_____

_____

CHALLENGE:

To transcend guilt and unhealthy obligation and do what you need to do to take care of yourself in order to better serve others. To hold rigid principles to judge others.

OPTIMAL EXPRESSION:

The ability to nurture yourself so you have more to give others. The intuition to know what others need to bring them into greater alignment with Love. To teach and share what you have to increase the well-being of others.

UNBALANCED EXPRESSION:

To overcare. To let guilt stop you from sustaining yourself. To hold to rigid principles and struggle to allow others to experience the consequences of their choices.

OCTOBER 21, 2025

NEW MOON

AFFIRMATION:

I am a powerful, loving force who loves and cares for my people. I know my capacity to give increases when I give to myself first. I have healthy self-care habits that fill my cup so I have more to give and am revitalized and resourced. I set clear boundaries and hold others accountable for their own self-care. My goal is to empower the people I love to be able to take care of themselves in abundant and beautiful ways.

OCTOBER 25, 2025

GATE 28: ADVENTURE/CHALLENGE

CHALLENGE:

Do not let struggle and challenge leave you feeling defeated and despairing. To learn to face life as an adventure. Do not let challenge and struggle cause you to feel as if you have failed.

AFFIRMATION:

I am here to push the boundaries of life and what is possible. I thrive in situations that challenge me. I am an explorer on the leading edge of consciousness and my job is to test how far I can go. I embrace challenges. I am an adventurer. I share all that I have learned from my challenges with the world. My stories help give people greater meaning, teach them what is truly worthy of creating, and inspire people to transform.

EFT SETUP:

Even though everything feels hard, I now trust that I am learning what is truly important in my life. I trust the lessons the Universe brings me, and I deeply and completely love and accept myself.

EARTH:

Gate 27: Accountability

Are you taking responsibility for things that aren't yours to be responsible for? Whose problem is it? Can you return the responsibility for the problem back to its rightful owner?

JOURNAL QUESTIONS:

◊   How can I turn my challenge into adventure?

◊   Where do I need to cultivate a sense of adventure in my life?

◊   What do I need to do to rewrite the story of my "failures?"

◊   What meanings, blessings, and lessons have I learned from my challenges?

◊   What needs to be healed, released, aligned, and brought to my awareness for me to trust myself and my choices?

◊   What do I need to do to forgive myself for my perceived past failures?

OCTOBER 31, 2025

GATE 44: TRUTH

CHALLENGE:

Do not get stuck in past patterns. To cultivate the courage to go forward without being stuck in the fear of the past. To learn how to transform pain into power and to have the courage to express your authentic self without compromising or settling.

AFFIRMATION:

I am powerfully intuitive and can sense the patterns that keep others stuck in limiting beliefs and constricted action. Through my insights and awareness, I help others break free from past limiting patterns and learn to find the power in their pain, find the blessings in their challenges, and help them align more deeply with an authentic awareness of their True Value and Purpose.

EFT SETUP:

Even though it is hard for me to let go, I deeply and completely love and accept myself.

Even though I am afraid to repeat the past, I now move forward with confidence, trusting that I have learned what I needed to learn. I can create whatever future I desire, and I deeply and completely love and accept myself.

JOURNAL QUESTIONS:

◊ What patterns from the past are holding me back from moving forward with courage?

◊ Do I see how my experiences from the past have helped me learn more about Who I Truly Am?

◊ What have I learned about my value and my power?

◊ What needs to be healed, released, aligned, and brought to my awareness for me to fully activate my power?

◊ What needs to be healed, released, aligned, and brought to my awareness for me to step boldly into my aligned and authentic path?

Gate 24: Blessings

Take some time to contemplate the hidden blessings in the painful events of the past. Can you find the bigger reason for why you've gone through what you've gone through?

MONTHLY REFLECTIONS

My wins from last month. How can I grow what I know is already working?

_____

_____

_____

_____

_____

_____

_____

_____

_____

_____

_____

_____

_____

_____

_____

_____

_____

_____

_____

_____

_____

_____

_____

_____

_____

_____

_____

_____

_____

MONTHLY REFLECTIONS

NOVEMBER

NOVEMBER

Monday	Tuesday	Wednesday	Thursday
3	4	5	6
10	11	12	13
17	18	19	20
24	25	26	27

Friday	Saturday	Sunday	To-Do & Notes
	1	2	To-Do: ○ ○ ○ ○ ○
7	8	9	○ ○ ○ ○ ○ ○
14	15	16	Notes
21	22	23	**NOVEMBER 2025** Mo Tu We Th Fr Sa Su 1 2 3 4 5 6 7 8 9 10 11 12 13 14 15 16 17 18 19 20 21 22 23 24 25 26 27 28 29 30
28	29	30	**DECEMBER 2025** Mo Tu We Th Fr Sa Su 1 2 3 4 5 6 7 8 9 10 11 12 13 14 15 16 17 18 19 20 21 22 23 24 25 26 27 28 29 30 31

MONTHLY INTENTIONS

Who will I be at the end of this month? Who do I need to be in order to fulfill my intentions for the month? How will I feel? What will my life look like? Write it out.

_____

_____

_____

_____

_____

_____

_____

_____

_____

_____

_____

_____

_____

_____

_____

_____

_____

_____

_____

_____

_____

_____

_____

_____

_____

_____

MONTHLY INTENTIONS

What key actions do I need to take to make the fulfillment of my intentions for this month my reality by the end of the month?

_____
_____
_____
_____
_____
_____
_____
_____
_____
_____
_____
_____
_____
_____
_____
_____
_____
_____
_____
_____
_____
_____
_____
_____
_____
_____
_____

MONTHLY READING

Using divination cards of your choice, pull three cards to help you set your intentions for the month.
Get your own Quantum Cards at: **https://quantumhumandesign.com/quantum-cards**

CARD 1

What influences and lessons from the past need to be mastered to support my evolution?

_____

_____

_____

_____

_____

_____

CARD 2

What is my overarching theme this month that I need to pay attention to? What lessons does this card
bring me?

_____

_____

_____

_____

_____

CARD 3

What do I need to strengthen and master to move forward?

_____

_____

_____

_____

_____

_____

NOVEMBER 5, 2025

GATE 1: PURPOSE

CHALLENGE:

To discover a personal, meaningful, and world-changing narrative that aligns with a sense of purpose and mission. "I am..." To learn to love yourself enough to honor the idea that your life is the canvas, and you are the artist. What you create with your life IS the contribution you give the world.

AFFIRMATION:

My life is an integral part of the cosmos and the Divine Plan. I honor my life and know that the full expression of who I am is the purpose of my life. The more I am who I am, the more I create a frequency of energy that supports others in doing the same. I commit to exploring all of who I am.

EFT SETUP:

Even though I am afraid that I am failing my life mission, I now choose to relax and allow my life to unfold before me with ease and grace. I trust that every step I take is perfectly aligned with my soul purpose, and I deeply and completely love and accept myself.

EARTH:

Gate 2: Allowing

How much good are you willing to allow into your life? Do you believe you can be fully supported?

JOURNAL QUESTIONS:

◊ Am I fully expressing my authentic self?

◊ What needs to be healed, released, aligned, or brought to my awareness for me to deeply express my authentic self?

◊ Where am I already expressing who I am?

◊ Where have I settled or compromised? What needs to change?

◊ Do I feel connected to my Life Purpose? What do I need to do to deepen that connection?

NOVEMBER 5, 2025

FULL MOON

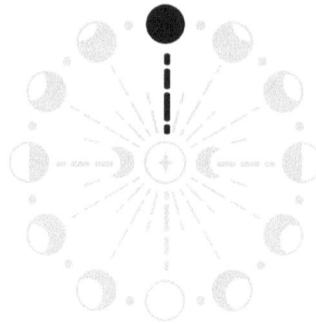

Taurus 13 degrees, 22 minutes

Gate 2: The Gate of Allowing

Full moon energy invites us to explore what we need to release and let go of in order to stay in alignment with our intentions.

There's a relationship between the New Moon and the Full Moon. The arch of the moon's transits from new to full represents a cycle of focused growth. This particular cycle, starting with the New Moon highlighting the Gate 21, brings us a powerful curriculum that hits many tender spots in the human story.

Since its emergence, we have been and continue to be taking the final exam in the curriculum the Will Center laid out for us. We've been mastering will power, healing our self-worth, defining our own value, exploring what we truly value, examining the relationship between our personal identity and our higher purpose, and transcending the footprint of history on our personal and collective narrative.

The New Moon invited us to look at what we need to regulate in order to create an inner and outer environment that reflects our true value. This Full Moon continues the theme by inviting us to reflect on the relationship between our perception of our value and what we're willing to allow ourselves to receive.

In other words, how much GOOD are you allowing yourself to have? Are you truly allowing all that you deserve? And if not, what needs to be released so that you can be fully open to all the support you need to live a genuinely fulfilled life?

CONTEMPLATIONS:

◊ What needs to be healed, released, aligned and brought to your awareness for you to allow yourself to be fully supported?

◊ What needs to shift in your perception of your value in order for you to allow all that you deserve?

_____

_____

_____

_____

_____

_____

_____

_____

_____

_____

_____

_____

_____

_____

_____

_____

_____

_____

_____

_____

_____

_____

CHALLENGE:

To love yourself enough to open to the flow of support, love, and abundance. To incrementally increase over the course of your life what you're willing to allow yourself to receive. To learn to know that you are valuable and lovable simply because you exist.

OPTIMAL EXPRESSION:

To set intentions and move solidly towards the fulfillment of the Authentic Self with complete trust that you are supported in being the full expression of who you are and your life purpose, even if you don't know how or what the support will look like. Trust in Source. Living in a state of gratitude.

377

NOVEMBER 5, 2025

FULL MOON

UNBALANCED EXPRESSION:

To experience stress and fear and ultimately compromise on what you want and who you are because you don't trust that you are supported. To be valiantly self-sufficient to the point of burning yourself out. To never ask for help.

AFFIRMATION:

I am designed to be supported simply because I AM. I trust in the infinite supply of the Universe and I relax knowing that I will attract everything I need to fully express all of who I am.

MERCURY
RETROGRADE CYCLE

November 9 - November 30

November 9 - Gate 9, the Gate of Convergence
November 14 - Gate 34, the Gate of Power
November 19 - Gate 14, the Gate of Creation
November 23 - Gate 43, the Gate of Insight

Retrograde cycles encourage us to go inward to explore the themes the planets give us. Mercury is the planet associated with communication. When Mercury goes retrograde it gives us an opportunity to go inward and contemplate how we can better align ourselves to have greater influence and impact in the world. Take your time to find the right words during this cycle. Do your best not to make big decisions, sign contracts, or make large purchases. Expect delays. Breathe and be patient with others (and yourself!)

We're in the middle of a cycle of focusing on work and money and redefining value and resources. This theme is being highlighted all over the celestial weather, and Mercury brings us a pause and a "mini-curriculum" highlighting the same themes.

It's easy to be distracted when we're overwhelmed, exhausted, and stressed. When we are afraid, our responses can become frenetic. We can get into our heads and try to figure things out instead of waiting to see what shows up and then optimizing our work.

Mercury reminds us that we are most effective when we simplify and keep moving forward. This is a time to ask yourself what actions you need to continue taking. What needs to stop? What needs refinement?

True power comes in response and is effective when we're prepared. Being focused and clear is an essential part of preparation. It allows us to know which are the right opportunities to respond to and makes sure that our response is effective and powerful.

We're redefining what creates true wealth. As things shift, this process of redefinition of value helps us continue to clarify what it is that we truly want. Mercury is inviting us to sift through the debris of the past and our dreams for the future and use the past to strengthen our dreams, our values and to clarify what we're willing to work for.

Expect to emerge from this Mercury cycle with renewed clarity, focus, and profound insights that promise to transform how you use your energy and where you're willing to commit your energy.

CONTEMPLATIONS:

◊   What are my dreams? What do I want?

◊   What do I need to do to stay focused on what I want?

◊   What distractions do I need to remove from my life?

◊   What key actions do I need to take to create my fulfillment?

November 9

November 14

November 19

November 23

MERCURY
RETROGRADE CYCLE

CHALLENGE:

Learning to tune out the fear and nay-saying of others. Trusting in your own inner knowing and inner timing. Pay attention and stay alert for the next right step. Keep yourself internally focused so that the external circumstances don't distract you.

OPTIMAL EXPRESSION:

To be deeply connected to your dreams and your values. To stay focused on what you want so you can recognize aligned opportunities when they show up. To simplify and streamline your actions so that you are most effective. To not let outer circumstances distract you from what's important.

UNBALANCED EXPRESSION:

Distraction. Lack of clarity. Pushing to exhaustion and wasting your energy on ineffective responses.

AFFIRMATION:

My focus creates powerful things. I am clear and aligned with my vision and my actions. I am intentional and deliberate with my thoughts and my actions. I take time each day to stay focused on my vision. I am moving forward and creating what I want.

CONTEMPLATIONS:

◊ What are my dreams? What do I want?

◊ What do I need to do to stay focused on what I want?

◊ What distractions do I need to remove from my life?

◊ What key actions do I need to take to create my fulfillment?

November 9

November 14

November 19

November 23

383

NOVEMBER 11, 2025

GATE 43: INSIGHT

CHALLENGE:

To be comfortable and to trust epiphanies and deep inner knowing without doubting what you know. To trust that when the timing is right you will know how to share what you know and serve your role as a transformative messenger who has insights that can change the way people think and what they know.

AFFIRMATION:

I am a vessel of knowledge and wisdom that has the ability to transform the way people think. I share my knowledge with others when they are ready and vibrationally aligned with what I have to share. When the time is right, I have the right words, and the right insights to help others expand their thinking, recalibrate their mindset, and discover elegant solutions to the challenges facing Humanity.

EFT SETUP:

Even though it is hard to wait for someone to ask me for my insights, I now choose to wait and know that my thoughts are valuable and precious. I only share them with people who value my insights, and I deeply and completely love and accept myself.

JOURNAL QUESTIONS:

◊ Do I trust in Divine Timing?

◊ Do I trust myself and my own Inner Knowing?

◊ What can I do to deepen my connection with my Source of Knowing?

◊ What needs to be healed, released, aligned, or brought to my awareness for me to trust my own Inner Knowing?

EARTH:

Gate 23: Transmission

Take stock of all the times you "knew" something even though you didn't know how you knew. Keep a running list of all your intuitive "hits." Start affirming for yourself how reliable your "knowingness" is.

NOVEMBER 17, 2025

GATE 14: CREATION

CHALLENGE:

To learn to trust and respond to opportunities that bring resources instead of forcing them or overworking. To learn to value resources and to appreciate how easily they can be created when you are aligned. To be gracious and grateful and not take for granted the resources you have.

AFFIRMATION:

I am in the flow of Divine Support. When I trust the generous nature of the Divine, and I cultivate a state of faith, I receive all the opportunities and support that I need to evolve my life and transform the world. I know that the right work shows up for me, and I am fulfilled in the expression of my Life Force energy.

EFT SETUP:

Even though I am afraid that I cannot do what I love and make money, I deeply and completely love and accept myself.

EARTH:

Gate 8: Fulfillment

What would your life be like if you felt relentlessly authentic? Do one thing this week that is an authentic expression of who you are without apology. Be bold.

JOURNAL QUESTIONS:

◊ Do I trust that I am supported?

◊ Am I doing my "right" work?

◊ What is the work that feels aligned with my purpose?

◊ How is that work showing up in my life right now?

◊ What resources do I have right now that I need to be grateful for?

◊ If I didn't need the money, what work would I be doing?

NOVEMBER 20, 2025

NEW MOON

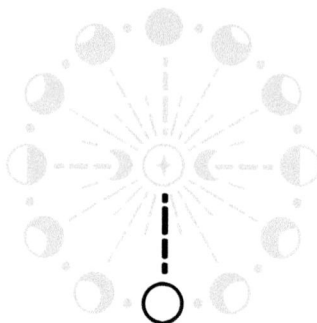

Scorpio 28 degrees, 11 minutes

Gate 14: The Gate of Creation

New Moon energy invites us to explore how we can deepen our alignment with our intentions and asks us to focus on what we want to grow and expand on in our lives.

The previous Full Moon asked us to expand on what we're willing to allow ourselves to receive. This New Moon invites us to explore our relationship with resources, including money, and to establish a new relationship between money and work.

We are taught that to make money or create resources, we have to work. If we want more, we have to work harder. When we trust in our own value and open ourselves to receiving more, we begin to realize a new relationship with our abundance that goes beyond simply working for money.

This aspect of money is rooted in the Sacral Center. With this transit we're encouraged to begin or deepen our pursuit of right work, the work that makes our souls soar and promises to support us in fulfilling our true potential. This is a place on the chart where abundance lives and our focus in this cycle is on money and redefining abundance. We're learning new ways to cultivate and define wealth.

In the shadow of this energy, we are dealing with scarcity, feeling powerless over money, and trapped in a definition of wealth that feels unfair and depleting. Money is simply a measurement of value. The more we increase our own perception of our value, the more we uplevel our relationship with money and right work.

CONTEMPLATIONS:

What needs to be healed, released, aligned and brought to my awareness for me to create a healthy relationship with money?

_____

_____

_____

_____

_____

_____

_____

_____

_____

_____

_____

_____

_____

_____

_____

_____

_____

_____

_____

_____

_____

_____

_____

_____

CHALLENGE:

To learn to trust and respond to opportunities that bring resources instead of forcing them or overworking. To learn to value resources and appreciate how easily they can be created when you are aligned. To be gracious and grateful and not take for granted the resources you have.

OPTIMAL EXPRESSION:

The ability to be at peace about having resources. To be in a constant state of trust that everything you need will show up in your outer reality in accordance with your alignment with Source. The resources you have allow you to increase the resources for others. To change the definition of "work". To no longer work for material gain, but work for the sake of transforming the world and being in the flow of life. To know that support flows from alignment with your Heart.

NOVEMBER 20, 2025

NEW MOON

UNBALANCED EXPRESSION:

Fear and worry about money. Being willing to compromise your "right" work to do whatever you have to do for material gain.

AFFIRMATION:

I am designed to be abundant. I am designed for work that fulfills me and aligns with my energy in every way. When I let go and allow, the right opportunities for me to fulfill my value and receive all the support I need to show up. Abundant opportunities surround me, and I train myself to see and embrace them daily.

NOVEMBER 22, 2025

GATE 34: POWER

CHALLENGE:

To learn to measure out energy in order to stay occupied and busy but to not burn yourself out trying to force the timing or the "rightness" of a project. To wait to know which project or creation to implement based on when you get something to respond to.

AFFIRMATION:

I am a powerful servant of Divine Timing. When the timing is right, I unify the right people around the right idea and create transformation on the planet. My power is more active when I allow the Universe to set the timing. I wait. I am patient. I trust.

EFT SETUP:

Even though I am afraid to be powerful, I now choose to fully step into my power and allow the Universe to serve me while I serve it, and I deeply and completely love and accept myself.

EARTH:

Gate 20: Patience

How do you manage the pressure you feel around the need for action? What are constructive ways that you can bring yourself into harmony with right timing? What do you do while you're waiting for the timing to align?

JOURNAL QUESTIONS:

◊ Do I trust in Divine Timing?

◊ What do I need to do to deepen my trust?

◊ How do I cultivate greater patience in my life?

◊ What fears come up for me when I think of waiting?

◊ How can I learn to wait with greater faith and ease?

◊ What do I do to occupy myself while I'm waiting?

NOVEMBER 28, 2025

GATE 9: CONVERGENCE

CHALLENGE:

The energy is about learning where to place your focus. When we work with the energy of this Gate, we have to learn to see the trees AND the forest. This Gate can make us seem blind to the big picture and we can lose our focus by getting stuck going down a rabbit hole.

AFFIRMATION:

I place my focus and attention on the details that support my creative manifestation. I am clear. I easily see the parts of the whole, and I know exactly what to focus on to support my evolution and the evolution of the world.

EFT SETUP:

Even though I have been frustrated with my lack of focus, I now choose to be clear, stay focused, and take the actions necessary to create my intentions.

EARTH:

Gate 16: Zest

Where have you sidelined your enthusiasm because others have told you "can't" do what you dream of doing?

JOURNAL QUESTIONS:

◊ Where am I putting my energy and attention? Is it creating the growth that I am seeking?

◊ What do I need to focus on?

◊ Is my physical environment supporting my staying focused?

◊ Do I have a practice that supports me sustaining my focus? What can I do to increase my focus?

MONTHLY REFLECTIONS

My wins from last month. How can I grow what I know is already working?

_____

_____

_____

_____

_____

_____

_____

_____

_____

_____

_____

_____

_____

_____

_____

_____

_____

_____

_____

_____

_____

_____

_____

_____

_____

_____

_____

_____

_____

_____

MONTHLY REFLECTIONS

DECEMBER

DECEMBER

Monday	Tuesday	Wednesday	Thursday
1	2	3	4
8	9	10	11
15	16	17	18
22	23	24	25
29	30	31	

Friday	Saturday	Sunday	To-Do & Notes
5	6	7	**To-Do:** ○ ○ ○ ○ ○
12	13	14	○ ○ ○ ○ ○ ○
19	20	21	Notes
26	27	28	**DECEMBER 2025**
			JANUARY 2026

DECEMBER 2025

Mo	Tu	We	Th	Fr	Sa	Su
1	2	3	4	5	6	7
8	9	10	11	12	13	14
15	16	17	18	19	20	21
22	23	24	25	26	27	28
29	30	31				

JANUARY 2026

Mo	Tu	We	Th	Fr	Sa	Su
			1	2	3	4
5	6	7	8	9	10	11
12	13	14	15	16	17	18
19	20	21	22	23	24	25
26	27	28	29	30	31	

MONTHLY INTENTIONS

Who will I be at the end of this month? Who do I need to be in order to fulfill my intentions for the month? How will I feel? What will my life look like? Write it out.

_____

_____

_____

_____

_____

_____

_____

_____

_____

_____

_____

_____

_____

_____

_____

_____

_____

_____

_____

_____

_____

_____

_____

_____

_____

_____

_____

_____

_____

_____

MONTHLY INTENTIONS

What key actions do I need to take to make the fulfillment of my intentions for this month my reality by the end of the month?

_____

_____

_____

_____

_____

_____

_____

_____

_____

_____

_____

_____

_____

_____

_____

_____

_____

_____

_____

_____

_____

_____

_____

_____

_____

_____

MONTHLY READING

Using divination cards of your choice, pull three cards to help you set your intentions for the month.
Get your own Quantum Cards at: **https://quantumhumandesign.com/quantum-cards**

CARD 1

What influences and lessons from the past need to be mastered to support my evolution?

_____

_____

_____

_____

_____

_____

CARD 2

What is my overarching theme this month that I need to pay attention to? What lessons does this card bring me?

_____

_____

_____

_____

_____

CARD 3

What do I need to strengthen and master to move forward?

_____

_____

_____

_____

_____

_____

DECEMBER 3, 2025

GATE 5: CONSISTENCY

CHALLENGE:

To learn to craft order, habits, and rhythm that support alignment, connection, and the flow of Life Force energy and the fulfillment of purpose. To become skilled at staying in tune with consistent habits and alignment that support your growth and evolution no matter what is going on around you. Aligning with natural order and staying attuned to the unfolding of the flow of the natural world.

AFFIRMATION:

Consistency gives me power. When I am aligned with my own natural rhythm and the rhythm of life around me, I cultivate strength and connection with Source, and I am a beacon of stability and order. The order I hold is the touchstone, the returning point of love, that is sustained through cycles of change. The rhythms I maintain set the standard for compassionate action in the world.

EFT SETUP:

Even though I feel nervous/scared/ worried about waiting for Divine Timing, I now choose to create habits that support my connection with Source while I wait, and I deeply and completely love and accept myself.

JOURNAL QUESTIONS:

◊ What do I need to do to create habits that fuel my energy and keep me vital and feeling connected to myself and Source?

◊ What habits do I have that might not be serving my highest expression? How can I change those habits?

◊ What kind of environment do I need to cultivate to support my rhythmic nature?

_____
_____
_____
_____
_____
_____
_____
_____
_____
_____
_____
_____
_____
_____
_____
_____
_____
_____
_____
_____
_____
_____
_____
_____
_____
_____
_____
_____
_____
_____

EARTH:

Gate 35: Experience

What experiences and stories from your own life do you have to share with others? Write a story about one of your favorite adventures you've experienced in your life. What did you learn? How has that shaped who you are?

DECEMBER 4, 2025

FULL MOON

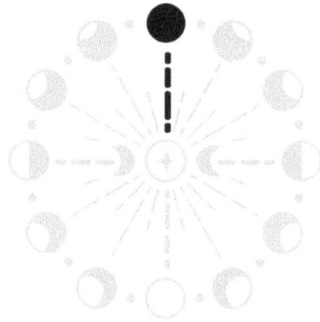

Gemini 13 degrees, 3 minutes

Gate 35: The Gate of Experience

Full moon energy invites us to explore what we need to release and let go of in order to stay in alignment with our intentions.

We're on the cusp of something new. Maybe you can feel it in the air. At the same time, it's been an intense year. We're exhausted, jaded, and maybe a little numb. It's easy to stop moving forward when we hit this kind of a wall.

There's a difference between being depleted and being jaded. Sometimes our lack of faith and lack of evidence that our dreams are being quietly constructed on the ethereal plane, can cause us to give up. This Full Moon reminds us to hang in there, encouraging us to rest and take stock of what has come before. The Full Moon wants us to trust the process and our own wisdom, even if things look temporarily challenging.

This same energy invites you to take some time to appreciate who you are and what you've accomplished and to stand strong in your wisdom. Your experiences are valuable and much needed by others who are just beginning. Where might you be holding yourself back from sharing your wisdom and experiences with others?

Lastly, the light of this Full Moon invites us to release anything that is holding us back from sharing and speaking out. Your experience gives you the wisdom to challenge the status quo and to integrate what you know with what is needed to move forward. Make sure you know the difference between the need for rest versus holding yourself back because you don't think what you have is important to share. What unique perspectives and wisdom do you need to share with the world?

CONTEMPLATIONS:

What needs to be healed, released, aligned and brought to your awareness for you to value the wisdom you have to share?

What do you need to do to *spark* your energy? Do you need rest? Do you need to break out of boring patterns

_____
_____
_____
_____
_____
_____
_____
_____
_____
_____
_____
_____
_____
_____
_____
_____
_____
_____
_____
_____
_____
_____

CHALLENGE:

To not let experience lead to feeling jaded or bored. To have the courage to share what you know from your experience. To know which experiences are worth participating in. To let your natural ability to master anything keep you from being enthusiastic about learning something new. To embrace that even though you know how to know, you don't know everything.

OPTIMAL EXPRESSION:

The ability to know which experiences are worthy and worthwhile. To partake in the right experience and to share your knowledge from the experience for the sake of changing the story of what's possible in the world.

DECEMBER 4, 2025

FULL MOON

UNBALANCED EXPRESSION:

To be bored with life. To let the boredom of life cause you to settle for a life that never challenges the status quo.

AFFIRMATION:

One of my greatest gifts is my knowledge and experience. My story is a story of inspiration for others. When I share my stories, it helps others know what else is possible for them. I value my experience and knowledge. I share when it's appropriate. I use my voice to inspire others and help them see other possibilities. My voice and my experience are a precious resource. The world needs my voice.

DECEMBER 9, 2025

CHALLENGE:

To learn to value your right place and your value enough to act as if you are precious. To heal past traumas and elevate your self-worth. To trust in support enough to do the right thing and to nurture yourself so that you have more to give.

AFFIRMATION:

I am a unique, valuable, and irreplaceable part of the Cosmic Plan. I am always supported in fulfilling my right place. I take care of my body, my energy, my values, and my resources so that I have more to share with the world. I claim and defend my value and fully live in the story of who I am with courage.

EFT SETUP:

Even though I am afraid to share my Truth, I now choose to speak my truth clearly and confidently, and I deeply and completely love and accept myself.

EARTH:

Gate 45: Distribution

This is a vital week to focus on what gifts you have to share with the world. How can you learn to give more without burning yourself out or martyring yourself? What do you need to do to increase your capacity to give and share?

JOURNAL QUESTIONS:

◊ Where might I be experiencing a breach in my moral identity, physical, resource, or energy integrity?

◊ What do I need to do to bring myself back into integrity?

◊ When I act without integrity, can it be traumatic?

◊ What trauma do I have that I need to heal?

◊ How can I rewrite that story of my trauma as an initiation back into my true value?

◊ What do I need to do right now to nurture myself and to replenish my value?

DECEMBER 14, 2025

GATE 11: THE CONCEPTUALIST

CHALLENGE:

To sort through and manage all the ideas and inspiration you hold. To trust that the ideas that are yours will show up for you in an actionable way. To value yourself enough to value the ideas you have and to wait for the right people to share those ideas with.

AFFIRMATION:

I am a Divine Vessel of inspiration. Ideas flow to me constantly. I protect and nurture these ideas knowing that my purpose in life is to share ideas and inspiration with others. I use the power of these ideas to stimulate my imagination and the imagination of others. I trust the infinite abundance and alignment of the Universe and I wait for signs to know which ideas are mine to manifest.

EFT SETUP:

Even though I have so many ideas, I now trust that I will know exactly what action to take and when to take it, and I deeply and completely love and accept myself.

EARTH:

Gate 12: The Channel

Spend some time this week contemplating what you need to do to deepen your connection with Source. Add some kind of creativity to your play and rest this week.

JOURNAL QUESTIONS:

◊ What do I do with inspiration when I receive it?

◊ Do I know how to serve as a steward for my ideas? Or do I feel pressure to try to force them into form?

◊ How much do I value myself? Am I valuing my ideas?

◊ Do I trust the Universe? Do I trust that the ideas that are mine to take action on will manifest in my life according to my Human Design Type and Strategy?

◊ What can I do to manage the pressure I feel to manifest my ideas?

◊ Am I trying to prove my value with my ideas?

DECEMBER 20, 2025

GATE 10: SELF-LOVE

CHALLENGE:

To learn to love yourself. To learn to take responsibility for your own creations.

AFFIRMATION:

I am an individuated aspect of the Divine. I am born of Love. My nature is to Love and be Loved. I am in the full flow of giving and receiving Love. I know that the quality of Love that I have for myself, sets the direction for what I attract into my life. I am constantly increasing the quality of love I experience and share with the world.

EFT SETUP:

Even though I struggle with loving myself, I now choose to be open to discovering how to love myself anyway, and I deeply and completely love and accept myself.

EARTH:

Gate 15: Compassion

Contemplate what old patterns in your life right now need to be healed and released. Take at least one grounded or symbolic way to commit to shifting and changing these patterns.

JOURNAL QUESTIONS:

◊   Do I love myself?

◊   What can I do to deepen my self-love?

◊   Where can I find evidence of my lovability in my life right now?

◊   What do I need to do to take responsibility for situations I hate in my life right now? What needs to change?

◊   Where am I holding blame or victimhood in my life? How could I turn that energy around?

DECEMBER 20, 2025

NEW MOON

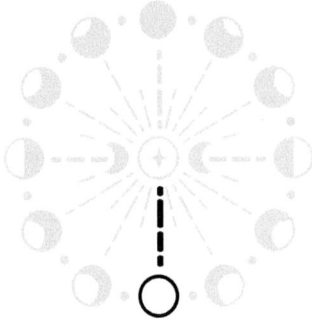

Sagittarius 28 degrees, 24 minutes

Gate 10: The Gate of Self-Love

New Moon energy invites us to explore how we can deepen our alignment with our intentions and asks us to focus on what we want to grow and expand on in our lives.

We've had a year of checking in with our higher selves and remembering to stay aligned with our higher purpose. We've been healing our self-worth and learning to act in accordance with our value. We've been rewriting stories that have kept us playing small and exploring what we deserve and need to support our authentic self-expression.

We're moving steadily towards the new year. (Interestingly, the Human Design New Year starts before we formally enter the first creative quarter for the year giving us one final cycle of reviewing what IS working and what we want to grow before we start doing the work of planting the seeds for the year ahead.)

This New Moon offers us the challenge of getting ready to start 2026 with our self-love strongly in place. What new identity do you need to establish to be a person who loves themselves wildly?

There is an important shadow side to this New Moon that we need to be mindful of. We tend to fall into victimhood stories when we don't love ourselves. We blame others for our circumstances and conditions. Not only is this wildly disempowering, but it keeps us stuck in old patterns that cause us to settle for and create less than what we deserve and want. Are there any new stories you need to write about reclaiming your power over a person, relationship, or situation (or yourself) under the light of this New Moon?

Remember, Love is an attractive and direction-giving energy. The more we love ourselves, the more our life takes us in a direction that aligns with Love.

CONTEMPLATIONS:

◊ Who do you need to become in order for you to be a person who loves yourself wildly?

◊ What new stories of self-empowerment and self-love do you need to write? (Literally, do this as a creative writing exercise!)

◊ What old stories of victimhood do you need to release? How can you retell the story in such a way that you emerge the victor?

_____

_____

_____

_____

_____

CHALLENGE:

To learn to love yourself. To learn to take responsibility for your own creations.

OPTIMAL EXPRESSION:

To see your love for yourself as the source of your true creative power.

UNBALANCED EXPRESSION:

To question your lovability, struggle to prove your love-worthiness, to give up and settle for less than what you deserve, and to blame others for your circumstances and situations. Victim consciousness.

DECEMBER 20, 2025

NEW MOON

AFFIRMATION:

I am deeply worthy of loving myself. There is no one else in the world like me. I make choices based on what is best for me. When I live true to myself and embody my self-love, the Universe rewards me with a life that reflects Love back to me. The Love that I am gives me influence over every area of my life. I am a victor and the creator of my own world.

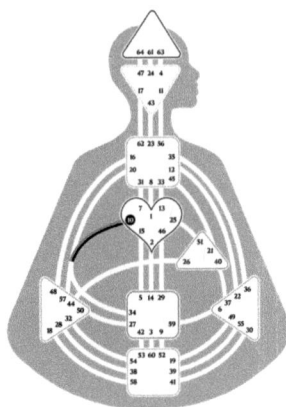

DECEMBER 25, 2025

GATE 58: THE GATE OF JOY

CHALLENGE:

To follow the drive to create the fulfillment of your potential. To learn to craft a talent and make it consummate through joyful learning and repetition. To learn to embrace joy as a vital force of creative power without guilt or denial.

AFFIRMATION:

I am a consummate curator of my own talent. I use my joy to drive me to embody the fun expression of all that I am. I practice as my path to excellence. I know that from repetition and consistency comes a more skillful expression of my talent. I embrace learning and growing, and I commit to the full expression of my joy.

EFT SETUP:

Even though it is hard to let go of the past, I now choose to release it and embrace all the joy that is available to me right now, and I deeply and completely love and accept myself.

EARTH:

Gate 52: Perspective

Is there anything in your environment or your life that you need to move out of the way for you to deepen your focus?

JOURNAL QUESTIONS:

◊   What brings me the greatest joy?

◊   How can I deepen my practice of joy?

◊   How can I create more joy in my life?

◊   What keeps me from fulfilling my potential and my talent?

◊   What am I afraid of?

DECEMBER 31, 2025

CHALLENGE:

To experience challenge as a way of knowing what is worth fighting for. To turn the story of struggle into a discovery of meaning and to let the power of what you discover serve as a foundation for a strong vision of transformation that brings dreams into manifested form.

AFFIRMATION:

My challenges, struggles, and adventures have taught me about what is truly valuable in life. I use my understanding to hold a vision of what else is possible for the world. I am aligned with the values that reflect the preciousness of life, and I sustain a vision for a world that is aligned with Heart. My steadfast commitment to my vision inspires others to join me in creating a world of equitable, sustainable peace.

EFT SETUP:

Even though things seem hard and challenging, I now choose to use my challenges to help me get clear about what I really want, and I deeply and completely love and accept myself.

JOURNAL QUESTIONS:

◊   Do I know what is worth committing to and fighting for in my life?

◊   Do I have a dream that I am sharing with the world?

◊   Do I know how to use my struggles and challenges as the catalyst for creating deeper meaning in the world? In my life?

_____
_____
_____
_____
_____
_____
_____
_____
_____
_____
_____

EARTH:

Gate 39: Recalibration

Where do you need to tweak your perspective to see abundance where you think there is lack? How can you shift the story to see what you have versus what you think you don't? Spend some time practicing reframing your perspective this week.

MONTHLY REFLECTIONS

My wins from last month. How can I grow what I know is already working?

_____
_____
_____
_____
_____
_____
_____
_____
_____
_____
_____
_____
_____
_____
_____
_____
_____
_____
_____
_____
_____
_____
_____
_____
_____
_____
_____
_____
_____

MONTHLY REFLECTIONS

JANUARY
2026

MONTHLY INTENTIONS

Who will I be at the end of this month? Who do I need to be in order to fulfill my intentions for the month? How will I feel? What will my life look like? Write it out.

_____

_____

_____

_____

_____

_____

_____

_____

_____

_____

_____

_____

_____

_____

_____

_____

_____

_____

_____

_____

_____

_____

_____

_____

_____

_____

_____

_____

MONTHLY INTENTIONS

What key actions do I need to take to make the fulfillment of my intentions for this month my reality by the end of the month?

_____

_____

_____

_____

_____

_____

_____

_____

_____

_____

_____

_____

_____

_____

_____

_____

_____

_____

_____

_____

_____

_____

_____

_____

_____

_____

_____

MONTHLY READING

Using divination cards of your choice, pull three cards to help you set your intentions for the month.
Get your own Quantum Cards at: **https://quantumhumandesign.com/quantum-cards**

CARD 1

What influences and lessons from the past need to be mastered to support my evolution?

_____

_____

_____

_____

_____

_____

CARD 2

What is my overarching theme this month that I need to pay attention to? What lessons does this card bring me?

_____

_____

_____

_____

_____

_____

CARD 3

What do I need to strengthen and master to move forward?

_____

_____

_____

_____

_____

_____

_____

CONTEMPLATIONS

JANUARY 3, 2026

FULL MOON

Cancer 13 degrees, 1 minutes

Gate 39: The Gate of Calibration

Full moon energy invites us to explore what we need to release and let go of in order to stay in alignment with our intentions.

As we come to the last Full Moon of the Human Design year, we have one final chance to release anything that keeps us from moving forward with power and intention. The previous New Moon invited us to explore our relationship with our self-love and sense of empowerment. This Full Moon invites us to explore the relationship between our self-love, self-worth, and our abundance.

We allow ourselves to create only to the degree to which we believe (or have faith). If we don't believe we deserve to create what we want or we don't believe we are worthy of support and abundance, we push our abundance away.

This Full Moon invites us to release any limitation that may be causing us to believe we don't deserve or aren't worthy of being supported and experiencing abundance. The light of the Full Moon is shining its clarifying energy on the shadows of limitation that live in our Hearts so that we can release and let go anything stopping us from trusting that we are infinitely loved, inherently valuable and deserving of sustainable support in every area of our lives.

CONTEMPLATIONS:

◊ What needs to be healed, released, aligned and brought to your awareness for you to have complete and total faith that you are fully supported and abundant?

◊ How can you strengthen your faith? What practices do you need to cultivate to sustain your faith?

◊ Do you need to deepen your relationship with Source? How can you better connect with your infinite support?

_____

_____

_____

_____

_____

_____

_____

_____

_____

_____

_____

CHALLENGE:

To challenge and tease out energies that are not in alignment with faith and abundance. To bring them to awareness and to use them as pushing off points to deepen faith and trust in Source.

OPTIMAL EXPRESSION:

The ability to transform an experience into an opportunity to shift to greater abundance. To see and experience internal or external lack and to use your awareness of lack to re-calibrate your energy towards sufficiency and abundance.

JANUARY 3, 2026

FULL MOON

UNBALANCED EXPRESSION:

Feeling overwhelmed by lack and panicking. Hoarding and over-shopping as a result of fear of lack. Provoking and challenging others and holding others responsible for your own inner alignment with sufficiency.

AFFIRMATION:

I trust in the path that is unfolding for me, knowing that every step is guided by a higher purpose and filled with divine wisdom. I trust in Source and know that I'm divinely designed to receive all the support I need to fulfill all that I desire. I strengthen my faith with practice daily. I take unlimited leaps of faith, knowing that I am fully supported.

JANUARY 5, 2026

GATE 54: DIVINE INSPIRATION

CHALLENGE:

To learn to be a conduit for Divine Inspiration. To be patient and to wait for alignment and right timing before taking action. To be at peace with stewardship for ideas and to learn to trust the Divine trajectory of an inspiration.

AFFIRMATION:

I am a Divine Conduit for inspiration. Through me new ideas about creating sustainability and peace on the planet are born. I tend to my inspirations, give them love and energy, and prepare the way for their manifestations in the material world.

EFT SETUP:

Even though I am afraid my dreams will not come true, I now choose to dream wildly and trust that my dreams will come true. All I have to do is focus my mind, trust and know that all will unfold perfectly, and I deeply and completely love and accept myself.

EARTH:

Gate 53: Starting

What identities and attachments do you have about beings, the one who starts and finishes something? How can you deepen your trust in right timing?

JOURNAL QUESTIONS:

◊ What do I do to get inspired?

◊ How do I interface with my creative muse?

◊ Is there anything I need to do or prepare in order to be ready for the next step in the manifestation of my dream or inspiration?

◊ How will I know when I am inspired? Will I feel it in my body?

JANUARY 11, 2026

GATE 61: WONDER

CHALLENGE:

To not get lost in trying to answer or figure out why. To maintain a state of wonder. To not let the pressure of trying to know keep you from being present.

AFFIRMATION:

I have a direct connection to a cosmic perspective that gives me an expanded view of the meaning of the events in my life and the lives of others. I see the wonder and innocence of life and stay present in a constant state of awe. I am innocent and pure in my understanding of the world and my innocence is the source of my creative alignment.

EFT SETUP:

Even though I do not know all the answers, I now choose to surrender and trust that I am being loved, supported, and nurtured by the Infinite Loving Source that is the Universe.

EARTH:

Gate 62: Preparation

This week's mantra: I am prepared. I'll know what I need to know when I need to know it. I know what to prepare when it's time to prepare it. I relax and trust in the flow. Repeat as needed.

JOURNAL QUESTIONS:

◊ What do I do to maintain my sense of wonder?

◊ How can I deepen my awe of the magnificence of the Universe?

◊ What old thoughts, patterns, and beliefs do I need to release in order to align with my knowingness and to trust my "delusional confidence" as a powerful creative state?

◊ What greater perspectives on the events of my life can I see?

◊ What are the greatest lessons I've learned from my pain?

◊ How do I use these lessons to expand my self-expression?

JANUARY 17, 2026

GATE 60: CONSERVATION

CHALLENGE:

To not let the fear of loss overwhelm your resourcefulness. To learn to find what is working and focus on it instead of looking at the loss and disruption.

AFFIRMATION:

I am grateful for all the transformation and change in my life. I know that disruption is the catalyst for my growth. I am able to find the blessings of the past and incorporate them in my innovative vision for the future. I am optimistic about the future, and I transform the world by growing what works.

EFT SETUP:

Even though it is hard to let go of things that did not work, I now release all the clutter from the past, and I deeply and completely love, accept, and trust myself.

EARTH:

Gate 56: Expansion

Tell yourself a story about your life, your future and your dreams that causes you to expand energetically. Allow yourself to truly fill up your energy field with expansion.

JOURNAL QUESTIONS:

◊   What change am I resisting?

◊   What am I afraid of?

◊   What are the things in my life that are working that I need to focus on?

◊   Is my fear of loss holding me back?

JANUARY 18, 2026

NEW MOON

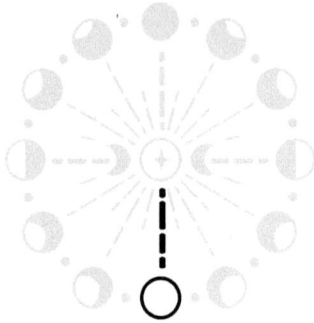

Capricorn 28 degrees, 43 minutes

Gate 60: The Gate of Conservation

New Moon energy invites us to explore how we can deepen our alignment with our intentions and asks us to focus on what we want to grow and expand on in our lives.

This last New Moon of the Human Design year, hovers between the very end and the very beginning of the New Year. This is a theme we've been playing with and growing through for the past few years through multiple planetary placements.

The Gate 60, Conservation, is the gateway to innovation. Forward momentum often needs to be tempered with contemplation and a careful evaluation of what is working in order to ensure that the way forward is effective. Gratitude is a powerful way to amplify what is working and allows us to innovate with ease.

The shadow of this energy is a fear of moving forward, a desire to return to "how things used to be," and conservatism that is blind to the potential of the future. The truth is,

we can never go back, but you can bring the good things from the past with you into the future. The fear of loss is reactive and causes us to default to old patterns. Gratitude is essential for momentum and can shift your focus from grief and fear to expansion of potential.

Research shows gratitude also supports higher states of creativity and Heart Coherence, better health and wellness and helps you build a foundation for momentum in all areas of your life. It's easy to get lost and focus on how "hard" things feel and the challenges of the past. Finding the blessings in the challenge and being grateful can exponentially catalyze growth and ease.

Use this powerful energy to set new intentions for the upcoming year that are rooted in innovation and momentum. You deserve an amazing year ahead!

CONTEMPLATIONS:

◊ What needs to be healed, released, aligned, and brought to my awareness so that I can fully tap into my inventive abilities and the energy to be resourceful?

◊ What am I grateful for?

◊ What IS working in my life?

◊ What fears about the past need to be released so that I can grow forward?

_____

_____

_____

_____

_____

CHALLENGE:

To not let the fear of loss overwhelm your resourcefulness. To learn to find what is working and focus on it instead of looking at the loss and disruption.

OPTIMAL EXPRESSION:

The ability to find the blessings in transformation. Optimism. To know how to focus on what is working instead of what's not.

UNBALANCED EXPRESSION:

To hold on and not allow for growth. To fight for the old and rebuke change. To let the overwhelm of change and disruption create paralysis and resistance.

JANUARY 18, 2026

NEW MOON

AFFIRMATION:

I am a powerful, inventive being. I always have the energy and knowledge to find creative solutions to whatever challenge I am facing. I use gratitude as my superpower and focus on what is working. I move forward with faith and trust in my total support.

MONTHLY REFLECTIONS

My wins from last month. How can I grow what I know is already working?

_____

_____

_____

_____

_____

_____

_____

_____

_____

_____

_____

_____

_____

_____

_____

_____

_____

_____

_____

_____

_____

_____

_____

_____

_____

_____

_____

_____

JANUARY

M	T	W	T	F	S	S
		1	2	3	4	5
6	7	8	9	10	11	12
13	14	15	16	17	18	19
20	21	22	23	24	25	26
27	28	29	30	31		

FEBRUARY

M	T	W	T	F	S	S
					1	2
3	4	5	6	7	8	9
10	11	12	13	14	15	16
17	18	19	20	21	22	23
24	25	26	27	28		

MARCH

M	T	W	T	F	S	S
					1	2
3	4	5	6	7	8	9
10	11	12	13	14	15	16
17	18	19	20	21	22	23
24	25	26	27	28	29	30
31						

APRIL

M	T	W	T	F	S	S
	1	2	3	4	5	6
7	8	9	10	11	12	13
14	15	16	17	18	19	20
21	22	23	24	25	26	27
28	29	30				

MAY

M	T	W	T	F	S	S
			1	2	3	4
5	6	7	8	9	10	11
12	13	14	15	16	17	18
19	20	21	22	23	24	25
26	27	28	29	30	31	

JUNE

M	T	W	T	F	S	S
						1
2	3	4	5	6	7	8
9	10	11	12	13	14	15
16	17	18	19	20	21	22
23	24	25	26	27	28	29
30						

JULY

M	T	W	T	F	S	S
	1	2	3	4	5	6
7	8	9	10	11	12	13
14	15	16	17	18	19	20
21	22	23	24	25	26	27
28	29	30	31			

AUGUST

M	T	W	T	F	S	S
				1	2	3
4	5	6	7	8	9	10
11	12	13	14	15	16	17
18	19	20	21	22	23	24
25	26	27	28	29	30	31

SEPTEMBER

M	T	W	T	F	S	S
1	2	3	4	5	6	7
8	9	10	11	12	13	14
15	16	17	18	19	20	21
22	23	24	25	26	27	28
29	30					

OCTOBER

M	T	W	T	F	S	S
	1	2	3	4	5	
6	7	8	9	10	11	12
13	14	15	16	17	18	19
20	21	22	23	24	25	26
27	28	29	30	31		

NOVEMBER

M	T	W	T	F	S	S
					1	2
3	4	5	6	7	8	9
10	11	12	13	14	15	16
17	18	19	20	21	22	23
24	25	26	27	28	29	30

DECEMBER

M	T	W	T	F	S	S
1	2	3	4	5	6	7
8	9	10	11	12	13	14
15	16	17	18	19	20	21
22	23	24	25	26	27	28
29	30	31				

CLOSING

CLOSING

Your Quantum Human Design is your key to understanding your unique energy, your Life Purpose, your Life Path, and your Soul's Journey in this lifetime. You are a once-in-a-lifetime cosmic event and the fulfillment of your potential and purpose is the greatest gift you can give the world.

I hope this year has been revolutionary for you and that you reconnected with the True story of Who You Are and the power and possibility of your very special life.

If you need additional support and resources to help you on your Life Path and Soul's Journey, please visit https://quantumhumandesign.com/find-a-quantum-human-design-specialist.

Here you can find Specialists and Practitioners who will help you understand the story of your Human Design chart, coach you, and help you get to the root of any pain, blocks, or limiting beliefs that may be keeping you from enjoying your Life Story.

Thank you again for being YOU! We are who we are because you are who you are!

From my Heart to Yours,

Dr. Karen

ABOUT THE AUTHOR

Karen Curry Parker, PhD, is an international Amazon best-selling author of multiple books on personal transformation, spirituality, and Human Design. She is the creator of the Quantum Human Design and the Quantum Alignment System™.

Speaking, coaching, training, and podcasting on these and other topics for 30+ years, she impacts lives daily worldwide. Her core mission is to help people reconnect with their natural creativity, manifest their desires effectively, and consciously use the frequency of language and narrative to craft a life that best serves themselves and adds more love and joy to the world.

With Quantum Human Design and Quantum Alignment System, she has created certification pathways for new and experienced coaches to add this transformative system to their business practices.

She has featured guests on her award-winning podcast, including Kyle Cease, Gregg Braden, Paul Selig, Dr. Joe Dispenza, and Dr. Gerald (Jerry) Pollack.

Karen is an eloquent speaker, well-versed in many leading-edge subjects regarding humanity's development and future. She teaches audiences engagingly and is adept at employing her sense of gentle humor to increase understanding and retention.

Karen holds a PhD in Integrative Medicine and is working on multiple new books. She is a faculty member at The Shift Network and Omega Institute. Karen has been featured on Bloomberg, Businessweek, CBS, and ABC, as well as various radio shows and telesummits.

To run your Human Design chart with the new Quantum Human Design language, go to https://FreeHumanDesignChart.com to learn more about Quantum Human Design please visit https://quantumhumandesign.com

For further inquiries please email support@quantumhumandesign.com.

QUANTUM LIVING
PRESS

2112 Broadway St NE Ste. 225, #305,
Minneapolis, MN 55413